UPDATED & REVISED

12
STEPS
TO BECOMING A MORE
Organized Woman

PRACTICAL TIPS FOR MANAGING YOUR HOME AND YOUR FAMILY

LANE P. JORDAN

HENDRICKSON
PUBLISHERS

12 Steps to Becoming a More Organized Woman: Practical Tips for
Managing Your Home and Your Family

© 2013 by Lane P. Jordan
Hendrickson Publishers Marketing, LLC
P. O. Box 3473
Peabody, Massachusetts 01961-3473

ISBN 978-1-61970-110-6

This volume is an updated and revised edition of *12 Steps to Becoming a More Organized Woman*, originally copyrighted 1999 by Lane P. Jordan.

Unless otherwise indicated, Scripture quotations are taken from the Updated New American Standard Bible®, copyright © 1960, 1962, 1963, 1968, 1971, 1972, 1973, 1975, 1977, 1995, by the Lockman Foundation, La Habra, California. Used by permission.

Scripture quotations marked NIV are taken from The Holy Bible: New International Version®, © 1973, 1978, 1984 by the International Bible Society. Used by permission of The Zondervan Corporation. All rights reserved.

Scripture quotations marked NKJV are taken from the New King James Version, © 1982 by Thomas Nelson, Inc. Used by permission. All rights reserved.

Scripture quotations marked NLT are taken from the Holy Bible, New Living Translation, copyright © 1996, 2004, 2007 by Tyndale House Foundation. Used by permission of Tyndale House Publishers, Inc., Carol Stream, Illinois 60188. All rights reserved.

First Printing — October 2013

Library of Congress Cataloging-in-Publication Data

Jordan, Lane P.
    12 steps to becoming a more organized woman : practical tips for
managing your home and your family / Lane P. Jordan.
        pages cm
    ISBN 978-1-61970-110-6 (alk. paper)
        1. Christian women—Conduct of life. 2. Women—Time management—
Religious aspects. 3. Home economics—Religious aspects.
    4. Housewives—Time management—Religious aspects. 5. Bible. Proverbs,
XXXI, 10-31. I. Title. II. Title: Twelve steps to becoming a more
organized woman.
    BV4527.J675 2013
    640—dc23
                                        2013025635

Dedication

This book is dedicated first to my husband, Scott, who partners with me in ministry as well as everything in my life. He is truly a gift from God. Secondly, to our beautiful daughters who light up our lives and baby Sara who shows us what true joy is.

And to my Lord, our Father Almighty, and to His Son, Jesus Christ, who through His Holy Spirit made this book possible. Without His wisdom, guidance, and perfect timing this book would not have been written and published.

ACKNOWLEDGMENTS

It takes a surprising number of people to make a book. This one exists because of all the friends and professionals who supported and helped me. I offer heartfelt thanks:

To Dan Penwell, who had the faith in this book to publish it the first time. Thanks for being there for me as the publishing process went along. To Michelle Rapkin and Barbara Greenman, thank you for the editing process. Your talents have made this book come alive!

To my friend, Marianne, who encouraged me to write this book, and to the other friends who promised to pray me through it: Lynn, Lossie, Kim, Lynne, Cathy, Judy, Sandy, Diane, Jill, Karen, Sharon, Rachel, and my Bible study group. To all of you, thank you so much. You are true gifts from our Lord.

"Many are the plans in a person's heart, but it is the LORD's purpose that prevails" (Proverbs 19:21 NIV). Thank you, God, for seeing this come to pass.

CONTENTS

Introduction   1

A Woman Who Wants To Become More Organized . . .

Step 1 Walks with God Daily   5

Step 2 Works Hard on Her Marriage   9

Step 3 Strives in Life Alone   21

Step 4 Reaches Out to Her Family, Friends,
        Neighbors, Church, and the World   41

Step 5 Understands Time and Its Importance   53

Step 6 Balances the Demands of Her Home
        and Career   73

Step 7 Stays Healthy and Fit   97

Step 8 Works to Provide Healthy Meals   119

Step 9 Manages the Details of Her Home   133

Step 10 Nurtures and Provides for Her Children   159

Step 11 Restores Herself Emotionally and Spiritually   189

Step 12 Seeks the Source of Her Strength   199

INTRODUCTION

When my publisher first asked me to revise *12 Steps to Becoming a More Organized Woman*, I was so excited! How wonderful to be given the opportunity to share and reach out to women again. But then I panicked. How could I develop new ideas or helpful tips that would be worthy of your time and mine? I didn't want to even think of a revision unless I could really add something of value.

Then I thought of all the changes—both social and technological—that have occurred since the book was published more than a decade ago, and my mind starting churning! I couldn't wait to get started and to share with you many of the organizational ideas and changes that have occurred since then.

Since the 1990s when this book was first published, our world and the ways we live, learn, teach, work, and communicate have totally changed. What caused this? First, I believe that our nation has moved away from "the faith of our fathers." Second was the development of computers and the commercialization of the Internet in 1995. The Internet has had a drastic impact on culture and commerce, including the rise of near-instant communication by e-mail and instant messaging, along with the World Wide Web, which offers us blogs, tweets, social networks, and online shopping.

It is estimated that in 1993 the Internet carried only 1 percent of the information flowing through two-way telecommunication. By 2000 this figure had grown to 51 percent, and by 2007 more than 97 percent of all telecommunicated information was carried

over the Internet. Today, it is almost 100 percent. Why am I sharing all this? Because as the world changes so do our lives. Many
of the tips I gave you in the first edition are either outdated or
can be updated. As an example, we don't have to send handwrit-
ten, stamped invitations anymore—we send e-vites through the
Internet! And we don't have to personally make phone calls to our
friends; we can just text them. We have GPS systems to help us
find where we are going, and we have phones that can also take
pictures and send e-mails. Why, our phones—and our iPads—are
now computers!

So how does all this help you and me become more organized? By understanding what's good and what's not so good
about technology and change. If technology is running our lives,
then it's not good. But if we can learn to use this new technology
to help us plan our days, then it can become a good part of our
lives. And that's why being more organized is so important. With
more data and more information—often too much—coming into
our minds and home, we can become so overwhelmed that we
end up not being able to do anything well.

I believe in a God who truly cares about every detail in our
lives, a God who wants our lives to be rich and full and complete.
He cares when a new mother needs sleep because she was up all
night with a little one. He cares when a marriage is on the rocks.
He cares when we have to juggle our home life with our work. He
knows what it's like to be hungry and not have the energy to buy
or cook food. He cares how we feel and He cares how we live the
life He gave us. He wants to give us "life abundantly." He says so
in John 10:10: "The thief comes only to steal and kill and destroy; I
came that they might have life, and have it abundantly." By studying His words and His ways, we can pull our lives together so that
they will be a blessing to us and to others, and a glory to our Lord.
It just takes the right motivation and a gentle push into being
more organized.

I believe that each of us has been created by God to be a unique individual. We each have different talents and abilities. Some people are orderly by nature while others are not. For those who aren't as organized, some of life's issues and stresses may be more difficult to deal with.

Many women struggle not only to be more organized but to simply keep up. There are more demands on women today than on my mother's generation. Because many women work part or full time in addition to raising children and trying to keep up a home, cook, and do laundry, they keep asking this one question, "How can I possibly do it all?" The answer is, "No one can." But we can learn how to organize our time and energy. We can learn how to prioritize our schedules and demands so that we can focus on the most important items first. Which brings me to the main point I want to share with you: Why should we emphasize being more organized? Aren't we already too busy to work on it? Yes, all of us are busy, and that's the reason I have devoted most of my career to sharing with women how to be more organized—so that you will have more *time* for those things in your life that are the most important: the Lord, your husband, your family, your friends, and those in need.

Along with teaching us the importance of time, the Bible shows that God "is not a God of disorder but of peace" (1 Corinthians 14:33 NIV). Order creates peace, calmness, and efficiency. In the beginning of the Bible in Genesis, God created one thing at a time, each on a specific day. He organized His creations until He was ready to create the best: us.

My prayer for you, reader, is that the information and tips I give in this book will encourage you to be more of the godly woman God has called you to be and motivate you to accomplish more than you ever thought possible. I pray it will help you organize your time so that your life opens up to a whole new dimension.

I hope you are as excited to start this new journey as I am. I am now a grandmother, so I feel I can share with you a lifetime of experiences, challenges, and joys. Since I have been a career woman, a married woman, a stay-at-home mom, a single working mom, and now a grandmother, I believe I can write and share with you from many different perspectives.

Here we go with Step 1 to becoming more organized. I'm so glad you are coming along!

A WOMAN WHO WANTS TO BECOME MORE ORGANIZED . . .

Walks with God Daily

*And what does the LORD require of you? To act justly and
to love mercy and to walk humbly with your God.*

MICAH 6:8 NIV

Our lives are so busy. Our world is so busy. Things happen now
in warp speed and I don't think it will ever slow down. We can
become lost in the whirlwind of demands. We don't just have the
mail to open and organize each day; now we have all the e-mails
to handle. We don't just have the notices from school to take
care of; we also have to check the status of our children's classes
online. Our children don't just have one sport practice a week;
they have a practice or game almost every night. Rarely are we
all together at dinner, as was customary in the past, because each
member of the family is off in a different direction. Instead of sitting together on the front porch or around a table playing a game,
most of us are in different rooms of the house, if we are even in
the house. And for many of you single women, the complexities
of life can truly be overwhelming as you try to navigate it on your
own. I believe that this busyness is the total opposite of how God
wants us to live, for it takes our minds off of what is important:

spending time with God. God created us to have a relationship with Him and Him with us.

Ever since Adam and Eve sinned, we have had problems in our relationships with God and with one another. I believe it's because at the root of our sin is our pride. Pride is what caused Eve to go her own way and eat the forbidden fruit. And pride is what caused Adam to throw blame at his wife for the sin. So is there any hope for us in our relationships? Yes! God sent His Son Jesus to show us the way, to bear our sin, and to bring us back into a right relationship with our Father. When we allow Christ to live with us fully, we can have that precious relationship with God. But we have to make that choice. God has already paved the way and done the work. We have to allocate our lives to Him—*we have to put God first on our priority list.*

One thing I am learning as I get older is that we truly cannot live this life apart from God. We think we can. We can even think we are doing all right. But in the end, when everything has been tallied, our life doesn't count unless He has been in our life directing it. Scripture states this as fact: "Apart from [Jesus Christ,] you can do nothing" (John 15:5 NIV).

As I look back on my life, I see many trails that have been rough and smooth, that have twisted around and then found their way back. Through all of these milestones, the only thing that kept me moving forward was my God. Apart from Him, I literally don't know what I would have done. I am thankful *every day* that God loved me enough to woo me to Himself and, thankfully, I called upon the Lord to save me.

Why would I start this book with this observation? Because I believe with all my heart that if we want to become more organized women who make a difference in our and others' lives, we first need to line up our priorities correctly. And the way to put God first in our lives is to walk with Him daily. How do we do that?

Here are some ideas:

1. Make the *choice* that now is the time to start putting God first in your life and in your daily planning.

2. Pick a daily devotional or a find a time when you can meet with God that works best for you and your schedule.

3. Realize that God is your heavenly Father. When Jesus taught the disciples to pray, He began with "Our Father in heaven" (Luke 11:2). This is one of many Scriptures that refer to God as a father. God wants us to know what He is like, and He chose to emphasize His Fatherhood. He is right there for you, ready to listen to your prayers.

4. Work on developing a "praise time" with God each day. Psalm 22:3 says that God "inhabits the praises of His people" (KJV). When we praise the Lord, He truly will be with us! A friend of mine wrote this about her own praise journey:

I've been on a praise journey, setting aside 20 minutes at least for praise every morning for 12 years now. My mentor first gave me the praise challenge 12 years ago when I was diagnosed with breast cancer and other areas of my life were falling apart. Most mornings I spend the time praising God before the sun comes up. The most effective way for me to do this is on my knees, in my office, with my headphones on listening to praise music and allowing the praise music to prompt my praise. It has changed my life! As I began to be intentional in this area of my life, I experienced the presence of God as never before. I am so passionate about praising God. When I need wisdom, I spend time praising God. When I need hope, I spend time praising God. When I need healing, whether physical or emotional, I spend time praising God. I have come to realize I can do nothing without worshipping Him. (Becky Harling)

Bringing home Step 1

You shall love the Lord your God with all your heart,
and with all your soul, and with all your strength, and
with all your mind; and your neighbor as yourself.

LUKE 10:27

For Further Reflection

1. Are you ready now to make the choice to put God first in your life?

2. Can you set up meeting times with the Lord on your calendar?

3. Have you found a devotional or study that will discipline you into a time with God?

4. Are you ready to join a Bible study or a church?

Personal Application

I believe that the only real way to strengthen any relationship is to start with the desire to do so. To begin a stronger walk with the Lord, look for practices that will help you do this on a consistent basis. Can you set up times on your calendar for your quiet times? Can you find a time where you can be alone and in a quiet place, apart from noise and distractions? Ask your husband or children to respect this time. All I know is that if you and I don't look for ways to change, we won't see change. I pray that your walk with God will become stronger and stronger each day of your life.

A WOMAN WHO WANTS TO BECOME MORE ORGANIZED ...

Works Hard on Her Marriage

The next relationship on our priority list is our relationship with our husbands. Our marriage is of utmost importance—God even compares His relationship with the church to a marriage.

I believe with all my heart that we need to make this relationship more important than any other, apart from our relationship with the Lord. God is the one who ordained marriage. When we bring honor to our husbands and put our marriage and family first, we are showing the world that we share God's priorities.

I know that the word "marriage" can be like a sword to some of your hearts. Infidelity, drugs, gambling, pornography, debt, and divorce have scarred many of us. When I first wrote this book, I thought my marriage was strong and stable. Then I found out it wasn't and it took me years to regain my footing. So I want you to know my heart is full of compassion for any of you who are struggling in your marriage. And for those of you who may be separated or single, the next chapter will address your concerns. But no matter how your marriage is, God wants you to place it as your number two priority in your life. Here are some steps that may help you in this vital relationship.

MAKE A DECISION

First, make a decision right now that you will place your husband above any others in your life. That includes your children, extended family, friends, and work. God will honor your commitment. I read of a young newly married woman who expressed her five-year marriage plan. Essentially, if she was still "happy" in her marriage at the five-year mark, she'd stay; if not, she would leave. Obviously, her goal was all about herself, rather than the man she had married or a lifelong commitment. My heart breaks at the immaturity of her plan. Happiness will always be fleeting, but true joy lasts a lifetime.

Remember that when building anything—whether a sports team, a home, or a marriage—we have to go back to the basics: to love, honor, and forgive. Establish shared goals and dreams with your husband, such as home ownership, children, or financial security. And make church a part of your lives. Glenn T. Stanton, director for Family Formation Studies at Focus on the Family, revealed that couples who regularly attend church divorce at a rate 35 percent lower than secular couples. In his book *Why Marriage Matters,* he states that "religious commitment rather than mere religious affiliation contributes to greater levels of marital success."

COMMUNICATE WITH YOUR HUSBAND

Next, it's important to learn to communicate with your husband. Today's marriage partners encounter obstacles not previously faced by other generations. Not only must they balance demands such as work and children, but also factor in the distractions of our high-tech society. From texting to e-mails, Facebook to Twitter, along with video games, the potential for losing your partner's attention grows each day.

Be available to talk to him day or night. After talking together, you may want to write down what the two of you would like to accomplish in your family, relationships, finances, work, and, of course, home. By setting goals, you'll be striving toward something instead of heading toward everything at once and nothing in particular. Your husband can be your biggest supporter and helper as you begin to organize your home and your life.

KEEP THE RIGHT ATTITUDE

Marriage is a partnership that requires teamwork, mutual respect, oneness, and intimacy. Your love for your husband should encourage you to act unselfishly toward him, looking out for his needs and giving of yourself. This does not mean you are to be subservient to him, but to honor him as your husband whom God has placed in your life to guide and love you. Many women are repelled when they hear, "Wives, submit to your husbands" (Ephesians 5:22 NIV). However, the verse preceding it shows the meaning of marriage the apostle Paul was trying to convey: "Be subject to one another in the fear of Christ" (Ephesians 5:21 NASB). Each person in a marriage is to give to the other in love and humility, respecting the position that God has required. The husband is the head of the wife (as a captain is the head of a ship), but he also is required to "[give] himself up for her" (Ephesians 5:25 NIV)—in other words, die for her. How sad for wives and families when both partners try to rule the other instead of submitting to each other!

When your husband asks you to do something for him, try to do it without complaining or forgetting. We truly do reap what we sow, and if we do something for our husbands with a sweet spirit, I believe they will do everything they can to help us. Of course, there are husbands who are difficult to live with! In that case, pray and ask God to honor your efforts. The way we act is so much more important to the health of our families and home life than we will ever know. In *The Living Bible*, 1 Peter 3:1 says, "Wives, fit in with your husbands' plans; for then if they refuse to listen when you talk to them about the Lord, they will be won by your respectful, pure behavior. Your godly lives will speak to them better than any words." Organize all aspects of your life so that you are there for your husband when he needs you.

Respect your husband's job and give him the time he needs to do it well. Try not to call him too often at work or complain when he has to travel. With some of the downsizing in today's workforce, our husbands need all the support we can give them. Pray for him to be successful in his job and for God to bless his efforts.

Never lie or be deceitful to him. This is also a great lesson for your children. My mother never kept anything from my father, and that taught us the importance of honesty, integrity, and faithfulness.

Recognize that you cannot fulfill all his needs. Encourage his interests in things outside the family. This may be hard when there are small children at home, but at minimum, work out ways for him to pursue his interests as well as help you at home.

Don't expect your husband to be able to fulfill all of your needs. No human being can meet all of another's needs, and just as you can't fulfill all of your husband's, neither can he fulfill all of yours.

Never try to come between your husband and his family and friends. Try to be a friend to his mother and never put her down or criticize her around your husband.

Don't forget to laugh! Let your marriage and your home be full of laughter and joy.

Find ways to WOW your husband every day! Pam Farrel has written a book that I highly recommend: *52 Ways to WOW Your Husband: How to Put a Smile on His Face.* If we shift our focus away from ourselves and toward our husbands, our marriages can be spectacular!

Be available sexually for your husband. This is such an important topic I should devote a whole chapter to it! My husband is in a men's accountability group, which is a group that keeps men faithful in all areas of their lives. They are "accountable" to one another and to God to keep from pornography, adultery, lust, and so forth. He tells me that one of the main complaints from the men is that their wives are not interested in sexual intimacy with them. In fact, some of their wives don't even spend the evenings with them, but instead are off with their own agendas. These men are lonely, hurt, and very available for the evil one to tempt them. Women, please love your husband in every way and keep your sexual relationship strong.

I would like to add one more thought since this topic is so crucial to our marriages. Dr. Kevin Leman wrote one of the best books on marriage I have ever read, *Making Sense of the Men in Your Life.* He writes that most men want to know that their wives want them. Leman says that the biggest sexual turn-on for healthy men is the emotional one (who knew that?!). He adds, "There's nothing like seeing your wife thoroughly enjoying herself in the midst of sexual relations. Realizing that you can bring your wife pleasure—even ecstasy—is tremendously fulfilling emotionally. It makes him feel like a man. Sexual fulfillment for a man requires far more than a willing wife. It requires an aggressive, eager, and fully engaged wife."

Work on ways to create intimacy. It's so easy to let some of the romance slip, but don't! Yes, there are days when your old soft t-shirt is the best thing to sleep in, but also wear a pretty negligee at times. Surprise him sometime wearing a coat and nothing else when you greet him at the door. Keep your bedroom clean and uncluttered, preferably without a TV or a desk. Keep your sheets clean and the bedroom smelling nice. Don't let your children sleep with you (unless they need to crawl in the middle of the night because of fears). Go to bed at the same time as your husband so you can have alone time to talk and be together.

Use technology to strengthen your marriage. Yes, I know that sounds counterproductive. Many of you have husbands who won't get off their computers or video games. But what if you suggested playing a game with him such as "Words with Friends"?

These games can keep you together by having fun. You can also Skype or have FaceTime with your husband, even if his office is down the hall from yours! My husband and I Skype with each other every time one of us travels. And sometimes, I'll Skype with him even though he is in the house with me! It's a great way to stay connected and share your love. Another idea is an app called IntiMate. Written by two psychologists, the app suggests intimacy-building exercises to do with your spouse, such as mindful attention and massage. Another free app, Icebreak for Couples, asks you icebreaker-style questions and then shares your answers with your spouse.

Do something for him each day. My mother gave me some great advice. She said that every morning when you wake up remind yourself to do at least one thing for your husband that day.

Remember to pray for your husband every day. This is one of the most loving things you can do for him. If you need extra motivation, try reading 1 Corinthians 13 at least once a week.

TAKE TIME TO LISTEN

Try always to be there for your husband. Care about his needs and listen to him. Be involved in his life. Adapt to his life. Remember, Eve was created to be Adam's helper. "Then the LORD God said, 'It is not good for the man to be alone. I will make him a helper suitable for him'" (Genesis 2:18 NIV).

Show a genuine interest in his work and in his hobbies.

Be respectful of his friends and be interested in them.

Occasionally, ask your husband his preferences. I have even asked mine what he likes and dislikes the most about me. (Note for the fainthearted: don't tackle that issue unless you're braced for an honest answer.) I really do want to know what my husband thinks and feels so I can work on any area that might cause a division in our relationship. His preferences will surface one way or another anyway; often the easiest way to learn them is in mature conversation.

BE AN ENCOURAGER

Do everything you can to build up your husband's confidence. Be his cheerleader and his encourager! Try not to ever belittle or criticize him. Don't be the enemy. Remember you married each other because you wanted to be together. Keep that thought with you always.

View your husband as a gift from God (which isn't returnable!).

Express appreciation to your husband freely. Let him know how much you appreciate all he does. Don't hold back the compliments.

It has been said that a woman's main need in a marriage is security and a man's greatest need is respect. Do all you can to show respect to your husband.

FOCUS ON HIS GOOD POINTS

Whenever you find yourself being critical of your husband, think back on how you fell in love with him in the first place. Rekindle those feelings and attitudes. Begin to love him again, to listen and be friends once more.

Be tolerant of his bad habits. Does he keep making a mess in the kitchen? Try to remember when he took all the kids away for an afternoon so you could have some free time.

Praise your husband in front of your children. Remind them that he is the head of the family and that all major decisions must first be approved by him. This will help teach your children respect and honor for their future spouses.

DO PRACTICAL THINGS FOR YOUR HUSBAND

Try to keep your focus on your most important job, which is to be his wife. It is so easy to get caught up in your job, your children, hobbies, or projects.

Find out what your husband would like for dinner and try to cook it.

Keep your checkbook balanced and don't spend over your means or your budget. He needs to be able to trust you with the family finances.

Keep yourself in good shape. I know this is difficult after the birth of a child, but try to keep your body fit, your hair clean, your clothes pressed, and your general appearance healthy. It honors our husbands when we try to look nice for them.

Spend a few minutes at the end of the workday catching up with each other and sharing news or events of the day. Don't entertain any distractions. Give each other your full attention.

Don't greet your husband at the door with problems. You both need some time to "decompress" a bit from a stressful day. Then when you do share problems, he will be more rested and ready to hear.

LET YOUR HUSBAND BE YOUR BEST FRIEND

Share your life with him first. Even though we have special girl-friends, our husbands should be our first and best friends.

Be ready and willing to share emotional, physical, and spiritual intimacy with him.

Play with your husband. Try to find activities you both like to do—and then do them. My husband and I love to take walks after dinner. It seems to be the best time to talk and be alone together. We also play sports together and swap books with each other.

WHEN THERE ARE PROBLEMS

If you are unable to act on any of the tips above because of a break in your relationship with your husband, ask God to love him through you. Sometimes only God can bridge the gap between you. You may need to go to a Christian counselor who can work with you and teach both of you some time-tested tools in conflict mediation. However, usually the problem is that one partner wants the marriage to work and the other doesn't. Marriages, and especially Christian marriages, are breaking up at an alarming rate. Evil is truly in full force, seeking who it can kill and destroy.

After speaking with women over the last decade, I have come to realize that no marriage is without its trials, pain, and heartache. You and I could try the rest of our lives to be excellent wives, with the end result still being a failed marriage. So, I have learned three things:

1. If one or both partners are selfish and self-centered, the marriage will not work very well;

2. If one or both partners do not want to work on the marriage, the marriage will not work very well; and

3. If one or both partners put their relationship with the Lord and their relationship with their spouse *last* in their lives, the marriage will not work very well at all.

My advice? Remember that "all things are possible with God." Fall on your face before the Lord, confess your sins, ask for a personal revival in your heart and soul and mind and spirit, and then pray—pray for yourself, your children, and your spouse. Never stop praying for your spouse, even if he leaves and you become divorced. The act of praying will help you to forgive and will hopefully one day bring another person into God's kingdom.

If you are experiencing any type of abuse—physical, emotional, verbal, financial, or deceit or betrayal—please get someone whom you can trust to help you immediately. God does not want His children to suffer like that. You will not be able to handle these problems alone.

According to the latest statistics, 25 percent of American women are the victims of domestic abuse. That means one in four women! The real numbers are almost certainly higher, since many cases go unreported because women feel shame about being in an abusive relationship—or have an unclear definition of what "abuse" is. As Dr. Phil mentions in one of his columns, "There are many relationship issues that can and should be worked through—and then there are absolute deal breakers. Any kind of abuse—whether it's verbal, mental, emotional, or physical—belongs in the latter category. If a woman feels threatened, her first priority should be creating an exit strategy to get to safety as quickly as possible."

There are many organizations now that can help families and marriages, such as the National Network to End Domestic Violence (www.nnedv.org), Focus on the Family and James Dobson's many books and recordings, Gary Smalley's seminars and videos, and Dennis Rainey and his marriage and family ministry.

My prayer for you, dear reader, is that your marriage will glorify God and give you much joy.

Love is patient, love is kind and is not jealous; love does not brag and is not arrogant, does not act unbecomingly; it does not seek its own, is not provoked, does not take into account a wrong suffered; ... [Love] bears all things, believes all things, hopes all things, endures all things. Love never fails.

1 CORINTHIANS 13:4-8

TEN RULES FOR SUCCESS IN MARRIAGE

1. Have a plan, some central idea, as definite a pattern for your life as possible and a clearly understood object for the joint project.

2. Remember that sooner or later money is apt to be a cause of friction.

3. Apportion your time and energy, allowing each to share joint homemaking duties, as well as individual responsibilities.

4. Let neither husband nor wife strive to be the dominating person in the household.

5. Expect to disagree. Two people may hold entirely different views on many subjects and yet respect and care for each other.

6. Be honest.

7. Be loyal. Keep your differences to yourselves. The less said about your married troubles, except between yourselves, the better. The feeling that many young married people have—that they can complain to their parents when things do not go just right—is bad for them and brings more serious trouble later on.

8. Talk things over. When hurt, do not keep it to yourself, brooding over it. Meet every situation in the open. Troubles that seem momentous quickly vanish when frankly dealt with.

9. Avoid trivial criticisms. Grumbling and complaints use up the vital forces of man or woman.

10. Keep alive the spirit of courtship, that thoughtfulness which existed before marriage. Look for traits in the other that can be admired and praised. You can accomplish much by stimulating self-confidence in your partner.

As for the inlaws, offer as little advice to the newly married couple as possible, preferably none.

—ELEANOR ROOSEVELT, 1931

Bringing home Step 2

Marriage should be honored by all, and the
marriage bed should be kept pure.

HEBREWS 13:4 NIV

For Further Reflection

1. What can you do to encourage your husband and build your marriage?

2. What tips from your own experience that strengthen your marriage could you add to this step?

3. What can you do to make your husband feel that you want to be intimate with him?

4. What changes should you begin in your own life that will help your marriage?

5. Do you put your husband before yourself in a way that honors God?

Personal Application

I know that marriage can be very difficult, but when both people are in sync it can be so full of joy! This week, begin to ask yourself what needs to be changed. Do you have a negative attitude toward your husband? Are you doing so much that you are too tired for him? Do you need to add an evening to your schedule where the two of you have fun? Can you pinpoint what you could do to become more of the wife you want to be?

The more emotionally healthy a person is the healthier their relationships will be. If you feel that you or your husband isn't healthy in this area, look into finding a marriage counselor. As we get healthier, so will our marriages.

A WOMAN WHO WANTS TO BECOME MORE ORGANIZED ...

Strives in Life Alone

The LORD your God is living among you. He is a mighty Savior.
He will take delight in you with gladness. With his love, he will
calm all your fears. He will rejoice over you with joyful songs.

ZEPHANIAH 3:17 NLT

Living life alone was never God's plan. He created Eve to be a helpmate to Adam and for Adam to be one to her. Our world, however, is no longer perfect. We no longer live in the garden of Eden, and marriages end and death occurs. Perhaps that's why this verse reminds us that we do need each other: "A cord of three strands is not quickly broken" (Ecclesiastes 4:12 NIV).

But in today's world, statistics reveal that there are more single women than married women living in the United States. The 2010 U.S. Census found that only 48 percent of all American households were made up of a married couple. This is a startling finding. In fact, the number of Americans who are living alone has shot up from 9 percent in 1950 to 28 percent today. In 1990, 65 percent of Americans said that children are very important to a successful marriage. Now, only 41 percent of Americans say they believe that. Our churches, neighborhoods, and social networks are still largely set up for the married woman. Yet in her book *Half the Church*, Carolyn Custis James reveals that single women make up a large proportion of church membership globally.

When *12 Steps* was first published in 1999, I added some tips for the single woman. But for this updated edition, we realized that the single woman needed a whole chapter! In 1999, I had been happily married for twenty-three years with children. By the next year, I was separated from my husband and was now filed under the heading "single mom." That was one title I never thought I would have. And that is just the point. One phone call from a hospital or someone else can change a woman's status in an instant.

Even if a woman marries and has children, she spends less than half of her life in this role. Once the children leave home, her role in the home is more as wife than mother. And since women usually outlive men, her status may change again from a married woman to a single woman as a widow. All this is to say that women need to be prepared to live as single women for *some part of their lives.*

Another fact: Women are staying single much longer now. They do not and should not feel that they are "on hold" until they marry and have children. Being married is not the only job God created you for! I want each woman reading this to know that you are needed by God to help fulfill the Great Commission that Jesus instructed us to follow and that you, and not your status, are what is important.

The church is called "the bride of Christ." Of course, that is a spiritual metaphor, and it may not be a huge comfort when you wish you had someone cuddling you in bed on a cold winter night! But it's important to remember that even though you may not be married, there is someone who cares about you like a husband. You may be physically alone, but be sure to remind yourself every day that you are not without resources for strength and support. In fact, God is more reliable than even the best earthly husband.

Below are different areas where being more organized can help you become successful in your life. Yes, there will be days when you will struggle and put in more hours than your married counterpart. But from someone who has been there, remember that God is stronger than any obstacle in our way—He is your mighty Savior!

FINDING YOUR PATH

One of the hardest obstacles I have had to overcome is trying to understand God's will in my life and patiently waiting to discover what that looks like. Yes, we are to live and grow into the image of Christ. But what are we supposed to do when it comes to finding a job, a career, or where to live? How are we to know whom to date or to marry?

I believe the best teacher and guide we can have is God Himself, His Word, and His Holy Spirit. Psalm 1 helps to pinpoint what we are to do daily. First, let's not let our decisions and choices be controlled by the "counsel of the ungodly." Second, we need to stay away from people and places "in the way of sinners," those people who don't know Jesus. Third, don't get comfortable with those who mock God, His Word, and His role in our life so that their thinking may seem right to us. Instead we need to get our training, our guidance, and our advice from God's holy Word and those who know it and love it. God says that the person who does this will be like "a tree planted by streams of water; . . . and in whatever he does, he prospers" (Psalm 1:3).

Next, start to track your passions. When was the last experience that made you forget that time was passing? Perhaps it was reading to your child or when you were in a library. Maybe you love to be outside and walking brings this joy to you.

As you begin to narrow down what brings you to life, look at your calendar and see if you can start deleting some activities that don't bring you joy and adding those that do. Over time, these little steps may lead to big changes. You may find a job where you can incorporate your passions into a paying position or giving yourself the time for them.

And please hear me at this point. Many of you are single mothers with small children, and you barely have the time or energy to make them dinner. I understand! But as you go about your days, begin to ask God to show you the little things in life that are joyful to you. God wants us to have "an abundant life," and this means that even without much money, we can live that kind of life.

FINANCES

I believe that the hardest part of being a single woman is trying to make it in this world on one income. From the single mom to the new widow, finances cause the most stress. In fact, more than a third of American women are now the family breadwinner. So let me share some tips here that I hope will help.

Don't bury your head in the sand. For some women, and even those with multiple degrees, money scares them. Taking a good look at their finances is a psychological hurdle. Why? Many women lack confidence when discussing money and investments. We can get stuck waiting for someone else to fix the problem. (Does the name Cinderella ring a bell?)

Talk with a financial planner. Even if you only make hourly pay, find someone you trust to help you *plan.* By planning I mean taking the time to save now for the future and to help you with many of the investment alternatives available today. Making your financial goals as detailed as possible will increase the likelihood that you'll do what's necessary to achieve them.

Be informed, not intimidated. Many women flee from financial planning because it scares them and they don't understand the language. If money discussions make you feel nervous or clueless, you have to start talking about your finances more, not less. Again, find a relative or someone you trust to help you.

Read the experts. There are many financial magazines as well as books to help you with your finances. Here are some that can help: *The Millionaire Next Door* by Thomas J. Stanley and William D. Danko; *The Investment Answer* by Daniel C. Goldie and Gordon S. Murray; *Charles Schwab's New Guide to Financial Independence* by Charles Schwab; *The Total Money Makeover* by Dave Ramsey; and, from one of the best writers for women, *The Money Class: How to Stand in Your Truth and Create the Future You Deserve* by Suze Orman.

Go online. Check out these web-based financial resources that are geared toward women: DailyWorth.com for smart tips and real-time money discussions with other women; and WomenandCo.com for advice on budgeting, investments, careers, and more. Also, you can join a women's money group. Check out the "Money Clubs" page on the Women's Institute for Financial Education website to find one near you. You should also pay your bills online. Set up a separate e-mail account to keep your e-bills orderly. Last, there is an app that organizes and tracks your money and bills and offers real-time alerts and reminders about bill due dates, overage charges, and suspicious activity. It's called Check and it's free on Apple and Android.

Go to back to school. Perhaps you could take a basic personal finance class. Many local community colleges offer these and some churches have classes by Dave Ramsey, a financial expert with a daily radio program.

Understand life insurance. When I was single, I started to worry about needing this type of insurance. Here are some good tips:

- You need life insurance only if there are loved ones who depend on you financially. Ask yourself, "If I die today, would everyone be able to pay their bills?" If the answer is no, you need life insurance. Or if there isn't any money for a funeral, you may need life insurance.

- Never buy life insurance on a child's life. Life insurance is financial insurance: its purpose is to replace needed income, and your children don't bring in an income.

- You probably don't need life insurance forever. Once your children are adults or you have ample savings and home equity to support your family, chances are you can skip it. Suze Orman recommends term life insurance that provides coverage for ten or twenty years. You can learn more at Accuquote.com and SelectQuote.com.

Make the most of your health insurance. The first rule is to stay in-network for your doctors and hospital visits. Don't skimp on screenings, immunizations, and other services your plan may provide, such as discounted gym memberships and wellness classes. Use generic drugs whenever possible. Set up a flexible spending account if your employer offers one.

There is no excuse for being ignorant about finances. For those of you who are reading this and are married or those who are single and planning on getting married, the last thing you want your husband to say is, "Honey, I'll take care of everything." Not every man is capable with money and you never know when your husband will either die or leave you. You must know your annual income and the cost of living for your family. You must know all your investments, saving accounts, checking accounts, insurances, and where all the financial records are. You must know where your retirement income is likely to come from. Both partners need to have a broad understanding of the finances, including husbands whose wives are the family bookkeepers.

Keep accurate tax records. Forget that shoebox full of paper. Try Shoeboxed.com instead to digitize receipts and store them online. You can also go to www.irs.gov or use the IRS2Go app, which offers tax-prep tips and tools. Another helpful app called IDonatedIt stores pictures of donated goods, estimates their value, keeps a running total, and lets you e-mail it to your accountant.

Be careful how you spend your money. Step back and look at the big picture. Fifty percent of your take-home pay should be allocated for essentials, 20 percent should go toward savings and debt, and 30 percent can cover everything else, like the 10 percent given to God as a tithe to your church home. Perhaps you could go on a financial fast during which you eliminate all spending except for the bare essentials. I do know that when we stop buying, we realize how much we consume that isn't important. You could also try keeping a spending journal for 30 days. A month's worth of data makes it easier to see where you can cut back.

Understand whose money it really is. Financial stewardship is about more than simply giving to the church. It's about spending every penny you have to the glory of God. Yes, we will have fun purchases, but the ultimate test of a purchase is understanding whether God is getting the glory or I am.

Remember that being financially smart isn't about having a lot of money. Millionaires go bankrupt every day. It's about understanding how to take care of money so that you have the power over it and not the other way around. If you are having trouble with your finances, start by asking God to help you.

Another good resource would be a financial expert such as Suze Orman who has written numerous books on personal finance, particularly for women. She wrote an extremely helpful article for *Oprah* magazine titled "The Best Financial Moves for Your 20s, 30s, 40s, 50s, 60s and Beyond: A decade-by-decade plan for securing your financial future" (January 2013). This can be found online at www.oprah.com, along with multiple other articles on personal finance.

One thing a woman should do is to keep an **emergency fund**. Yes, if the unexpected happens, you could always use your credit cards, but financial planners say there are five vital reasons you should keep a special fund just for emergencies, even if you only have the funds in a savings account that pays almost zero interest:

1. You might lose your job. If you put expenses on your credit card and then lose your job it can be disastrous. You don't want your credit rating to go down either.

2. You might become injured or sick. Even if you have excellent health insurance, you may need this fund for unexpected expenses while you recuperate.

3. The emergency fund helps diversify your assets. You never want to put all your money in one place. This fund contains money you can access quickly.

4. Cash is accepted everywhere. In an emergency, some places don't accept credit cards.

5. You will sleep better! Having an emergency fund will give you peace of mind.

To end this section on finances, I wanted to add just a few tips on working. Most of us will always have to work, especially if we are single. And finding the right job as well as being the right worker is crucial for you to have long-term success. Perhaps you dislike your job but feel it's your only option right now. More than likely, you fall somewhere in the middle. Whatever the case, these tips may help you feel happier at work.

Tackle difficult tasks first. It's human nature to put off an unpleasant phone call or a high-pressure task, only to find it looming larger in your mind. Rather than allowing a task to hang over you and drag down your mood all day, bite the bullet and get it over with.

Get outside. Fluorescent lights can zap your energy and spirit—especially during the winter when you may be arriving and leaving work in the dark. Nothing refreshes the human mind, body, and spirit like a little fresh air and seeing nature. Make a habit to walk outside during your breaks or lunch hour.

Organize and spruce up your work space. Surround yourself with things that make you feel happy like pictures of your loved ones, green plants, or even pillows for a chair. Find extra trays or files so you can clear your desktop for only what you need the majority of the time.

Have an attitude of gratitude. Yes, it's easy to complain about your manager (I have!) and all the things you dislike about your job. Begin your days considering the things you like about your job or, at least, your life. The items on your list can be as big or as small as you want. When you focus on the positive and remember to have a grateful heart, your work day will turn for the better.

Being happy is a decision, so dwell on the aspects of your work that you like. Avoid negative coworkers. Compliment others on the job they're doing. Make a conscious choice to be positive, no matter what comes your way. And if you need encouragement, remember that Joseph was sold into slavery by his very own brothers but rose to become the most powerful man in Egypt because he trusted in God.

PARENTING

Being a single parent is just plain hard. You have two fewer hands to help with everything. You don't have another adult in the home to have a real conversation with or to help you carry the load. There are now 11.3 million one-parent families in the U.S., up 13.8 percent from 2002, according to the U.S. Census Bureau. If you're in that group, here's what you need to know.

Create a budget. As I mentioned earlier, single women and especially single moms need to preserve financial stability, since they are the sole income earner. Todd Mark, vice president of education at Consumer Credit Counseling Service, advises, "When determining your budget after the loss of a spouse, ruthlessly cut your standard of living until you are spending less than you earn. The children will adjust much more easily than you think." And make sure the children know what the budget is and then stick to it. If they want to break the budget, make sure they understand they have to give up something else. One positive aspect of this budget is that you are teaching your children at an early age that money does not grow on trees. It takes hard work and smart living to have it.

Don't feel guilty. Please don't let single-parent guilt make you buy expensive items or relax the discipline children need. I feel that guilt is one of the strongest emotions a single mom experiences, whether she has anything to feel guilty about or not. Yes, your children have lost their father, but consoling them by giving whatever they want is not the right path. The one thing your children need is you along with a peaceful home environment. If you are upset emotionally, perhaps they can stay with a grandparent until you can get the help you need. Yes, it's okay to cry in front of your children. They need to know that when there is a loss (death or divorce), grief is a way to handle it. But we also need to get the help we need to get back in balance.

Also, realize that "mommy guilt" comes from the expectation that we need to be a perfect parent. But guess what? A perfect mom doesn't exist. God just asks us to do our best. Please forgive yourself whenever you fail. A defeated parent doesn't parent effectively. When we barrage ourselves with negative self-talk over a poor parenting choice, we continue down a negative path. Forgiving ourselves and giving our situation over to God allows us to begin again with a renewed mind and fresh perspective for our parenting challenges.

Teach your children. Yes, being a single parent is hard. But you still have to teach your children all that they need to know. Don't let your situation keep you from being their parent in every way. This is also a time when you will have to sacrifice. You may want to join your office workers for dinner after work or go to the gym. But if you have children, even teenagers, at home waiting for you, they are your first priority. You will have to make arrangements when you want to do something on your own.

And listen to your heart when you are facing a difficult parenting moment or discipline. Our job is to teach our children to become self-sufficient adults when they leave home. Being a single mom will force you to delegate more to your children, which is a good thing. And God is there to help you in every situation.

Be ready to seek organizations and people who can help you. Your local church, The Boys and Girls Clubs of America, Focus on the Family, and www.CBN.com/family are avenues where you may be able to find the help and advice you need. Another is our next topic: your friends.

FRIENDSHIPS

Having a friend is one of the best gifts from God. Friends are there to hold us up when life is trying to bring us down. I know finding friends can be hard. I had just moved to Texas when my husband and I separated, and I had no support group, no family, and no friends. I didn't even know my neighbors very well. Saying that this was a difficult time in my life is an understatement! But I did know that I needed friends, so I started to look for them.

Reach out to others. Whether you are going through your husband's death or a divorce, you may not feel like reaching out to others. But that's the very thing you need to do. If you already have friends, let them help you. Yes, you may prefer to be alone, but God places friends in your life for such a time as this. Is there a Mom to Mom or MOPS group at your church where you could meet other women who can help you? Could you join a singles Sunday school class or Life Group in your church?

One idea is to create your own circle of single women! Becky Aikman, after losing her husband in her 40s, couldn't find what she needed in a traditional support group. So she created her own group of women who relied on friendship, practical help, and laughter to help themselves heal. She wrote a book called *Saturday Night Widows* about her experience. Here is an excerpt:

We would meet on Saturday night, the most treacherous shoal for new widows, where untold spirits have sunk into gloom. We would do something together that we enjoyed, starting small—this dinner would certainly qualify—and ending big, maybe a faraway trip. . . . If nothing else, these women would provide each other with traveling companions past the milestones of this common but profound transition as the first holidays without a mate, the first time taking off the ring, the first time daring to flirt. We would converge at this most vulnerable, weak, and awkward turning point and pledge to each other that this was not an end, it was a beginning.

There may be groups that have already been formed in your community, or perhaps you could start one yourself. Another group, Wacco, was formed when a widow realized she needed a support group:

Wacco stands for Women Alone Cooperative Community Organization. The idea came about because soon after I moved to Connecticut with my husband, we bought a house and he died suddenly. I hardly knew anyone, but did know a few single ladies. I found myself (a) wanting to have companionship for dinners and (b) wanting to have the names of workers who could help me with house projects—plumbers, electricians, cleaning people, painters.

So I gathered as many single women as I could find in my living room and we felt we had a lot in common, even though we were from different backgrounds and professions. We put together a list of workers that the group had used and voted. And we would call around to each other if we needed something. We would take each other to airports, and do other favors which would be reciprocated.

But the companionship was the best of all. We had dinner at a local restaurant every Wednesday night, and whoever would like to, just showed up. And of course new friendships were formed so that during the week we could call on each other for more dining together. That worked so well and was fun to boot.

We would meet once a month in a different person's home. Sometimes we had a topic and/or a speaker. Once we had someone from an insurance company come and talk to us about long term healthcare. He asked if we were an organization, because if we were, we could get a group discount on that insurance. I asked what we would need to be an "organization." He said you have to collect dues! So then and there I asked everyone to contribute $1.00, and we were an organization. Later, someone wanted to really get us "organized" and have a printed mission statement. That was shot down. We liked the informality and companionship and information. We didn't want to muck things up with rules and regulations.

One of the funny things was that some of our married lady friends wanted to join us occasionally, but we were pretty tough about that. After all, the whole point was that we were single women helping other single women. However, we did let one friend join us for the year her husband lived and worked in New York! She loved coming to our dinners. She used to joke that she wasn't so sure she wanted her husband to come back—he did on weekends—because she loved being a Wacco! (Reprinted with kind permission.)

Pursue activities. Look for activities outside the home that will make you get up, get dressed, and get out the door. Depression is real, and sometimes just getting dressed can help keep it away. Is there an activity at your church you can be part of, like joining the choir or teaching? Is there a hobby you could now pursue, like painting or a sport? Perhaps you could ask a neighbor to walk with you every day. I just know that passionate pursuits in life are essential, whether you are single or not.

Making time for yourself is not selfish. Yes, if you have children at home this will be much more difficult. But you have to take care of yourself in order to help others. Now is the time to figure out what nourishes you mentally, emotionally, physically, and spiritually. Having a friend to bring balance to your life can help you achieve this.

TAKE CARE OF YOURSELF

When I became single, it was the last thing I ever thought would happen to me. I went from being a busy married mother of two to a single mom looking for work. Depression hit me hard. If you are experiencing a similar darkness, taking care of yourself is so important. Here are some tips I hope will help.

Visit your doctor. If you are experiencing depression, weight loss or gain, or other medical problems, let your doctor know. He may be able to give you ideas for proper nutrition, medicines, or places where you can get help.

Make your bed first thing every morning. Women of Faith speaker Patsy Clairmont was so depressed she couldn't leave her house. Then one day she heard a voice say, "Make your bed." Although she didn't have the energy, she obeyed and made her bed. From that day on, she became stronger as she began doing one more thing each day.

Take time to stretch. Studies have shown that by stretching our muscles, we are able to stand up straighter and perform better. It is also a way to slow yourself down and concentrate on your breathing. Yoga or Pilates are ways to help you.

Lift heavy objects. Yes, like weights! But you can also lift laundry detergent, baskets of clothes, heavy groceries, and babies. Our muscles decline as we age. So whether you are in a weight room or in your home, concentrate on lifting items as much as you can.

Don't forget to walk. To restore ourselves physically, we must move our bodies. By walking an extra 2,000 steps each day—about a mile—you can burn an extra 100 calories. If you combine that with eliminating 100 calories each day—maybe by leaving some food on your plate—you can prevent the one to three pounds of weight gain that most Americans experience every year.

Find time each day to rest. To restore ourselves correctly, we must rest. God wants us to! He gave us the commandment to keep the Sabbath and to stop our labor. Perhaps each day you can find ten minutes to sit, prop your feet up and rest, either by reading or actually closing your eyes. Take naps on Sunday or other days if you can. And most importantly, go to bed at a decent time each night. We need eight to nine hours of sleep a night. (*Note: See Step 11 for more help on restoring yourself emotionally and spiritually.*)

SIMPLIFY YOUR LIFE

Being a single woman in today's world can be difficult, but if you learn how to simplify and organize the different aspects of your life, you will have more peace and confidence. Have someone you trust help you. This person needs to have another set of keys to your house and car, to know where your important papers are, and what to do in case of a medical emergency. You also need to find a reliable helper for home repairs and help with the yard. I found a wonderful handyman from a flyer. The company was privately owned by a husband and wife and the workers were fully insured and bonded. And, of course, try to find a babysitter you can trust to help you with your children.

I know sometimes it can be extremely hard to find these people, but pray and ask God to lead you to them. One of my favorite verses is: "A father of the fatherless and a judge for the widows is God in His holy habitation. God makes a home for the lonely" (Psalm 68:56).

If you are an elderly single woman, do you have a medical alert item that you can call for help? Does your family or a friend know where your important papers are? Can you visit some assisted living homes near you in case one day you may need to go there? My mother-in-law had a minor operation, but because she was unable to use her arm, she couldn't use her walker and had to go to a rehabilitation home. Since that happened, she has now visited the assisted living homes in her area and realizes she may have to go there one day. She has also found a company who sends out workers to help the elderly in their homes, and the ladies sent to her have been wonderful. I know these are tough issues, but each one of us needs someone in our life who can be called on in case of an emergency.

Another way to simplify your life is organization—the main purpose of each step in this book. We need to streamline our lives, clear out the clutter, and reduce what we don't need anymore. When we have less clutter, our lives can open up to more peace and more time.

To end this chapter, I want to share some examples of single women in the Bible. Yes, there were some! In the book of Genesis, we see how God protected Hagar, Sarah's Egyptian maid. Sarah gave Hagar to her husband Abraham to conceive a child for them. This actually was a custom in those days when a wife couldn't bear children. However, after Hagar conceived and bore a son, she became insolent to Sarah and mocked her. Sarah, in anger, had Abraham drive Hagar and her son Ishmael away into the desert. Hagar was at the point of death when an angel of the Lord appeared to her and showed her a well of water. Genesis

21:20 says that "God was with the lad, and he grew; and he lived in the wilderness and became an archer."

Later in Genesis, we see how God found a husband for the young and single Rebekah by sending Abraham's servant back to the land of his birth (Genesis 24). The servant was wise enough to pray beforehand, asking God to reveal who the bride for Abraham's son, Isaac, would be. And Rebekah was wise to reach out to the stranger and offer hospitality to him and his camels. The end result is that the servant saw his prayer answered in Rebekah and took her back to marry Isaac.

God was also with the widows Naomi and Ruth in the book of Ruth. When she followed her mother-in-law Naomi back to the land of Israel, Ruth's chance of marrying again was very low. But she wanted to follow Naomi's God and so went with her. When you read this story in the Bible, you will see how God brought a kinsman redeemer, Boaz, to rescue Ruth and marry her. From their union came Obed, the grandfather of King David, in the lineage of Jesus Christ.

In the book of Esther, the original Cinderella story unfolds! God takes an unknown Israelite, Esther, and places her in a beauty contest where the winner marries the king. Remember, God is always working behind the scenes, for when one of the king's officials tried to eradicate the Jews from the land, Esther was the right person at the right time to halt it.

In the New Testament, Timothy was a disciple of and co-writer with the apostle Paul. He joined Paul on his second missionary journey and became like a son to Paul. This godly man was raised by his mother and grandmother, who shared their faith with Timothy: "I am reminded of your sincere faith, which first lived in your grandmother Lois and in your mother Eunice and, I am persuaded, now lives in you also" (2 Timothy 1:5 NIV). There is no mention of his father, so these women may very well have been widows.

And, of course, Mary, the mother of Jesus, was probably a widow. But God provided for her! From the cross Jesus called out to His disciple John and entrusted him with His mother and His mother with him: "He said to His mother, 'Woman, behold your son!' Then He said to the disciple, 'Behold, your mother!' And from that hour the disciple took her into his own household" (John 19:26–27).

Although I don't know your particular situation or how God may work in your life, one thing I know for sure: God knows! He wants to be your Lord, your husband, and your God.

> *For your husband is your Maker,*
> *Whose name is the Lord of hosts;*
> *And your Redeemer is the Holy One of Israel,*
> *Who is called the God of all the earth.*
> *"For the Lord has called you, like a wife forsaken*
> *and grieved in spirit,*
> *Even like a wife of one's youth when she is rejected,"*
> *says your God.*
>
> **ISAIAH 54:5-6**

Bringing home Step 3

A father to the fatherless, a defender of widows,
is God in his holy dwelling.
God sets the lonely in families.

PSALM 68:5-6 NIV

This chapter on single women is so important. I pray that those of you who are single understand that you have a special place in the heart of God! He wants to provide for you, protect you, and stand by you.

For Further Reflection

1. Do you have some ideas to help you find your way on this new path of life?

2. How are you doing with your finances? Do you have someone you can trust to help you?

3. Do you have a budget along with retirement plans?

4. Is there someone who can help you with your children?

5. Have you been able to find other single friends and activities?

Personal Application

Review where you are right now in your life. Are there areas that you may need to work on? Are there areas where you feel you have succeeded?

I understand if you are at a point in your life where you are devastated and you don't have the energy to start making new decisions. I understand since I have been in the same situation. So begin to pray and ask God to lead you and to show you the way. I promise He will.

A WOMAN WHO WANTS TO BECOME MORE ORGANIZED ...

Reaches Out to Her Family, Friends, Neighbors, Church, and the World

*You are the light of the world.... Let your light shine
before men, that they may see your good works
and glorify your Father who is in heaven.*

MATTHEW 5:14-16

Walking with the Lord, building our marriages, and learning to live as a single woman are important areas of our lives. But we also need to reach out to our extended family. This category comprises our mothers and fathers, grandmothers and grandfathers, sisters and brothers, in-laws, aunts and uncles, cousins, and nieces and nephews. When we are more organized, we will have the time and the capacity to serve these special people in our lives. And I also believe that when we have people in our lives that need us, we will be forced to become more organized so we can help them.

Try to remember birthdays and anniversaries. Call when you can or write letters if you live out of town from them.

Be available for family dinners or get-togethers. Your extended family should be an important part of your life.

When a need comes up, rally around that family member and do all you can to help, especially the sick, the aged, and those with financial problems. Elderly parents who become sick and helpless can be difficult for their middle-aged children. These children are called the "sandwich generation" because they are caught between their children who need them and their aged parents who need them. The exhaustion and helplessness they feel can be overwhelming. If you are in this situation, go to your pastor or others for help. Remember to pray. God will give you the strength to get through it.

REACH OUT TO YOUR FRIENDS

I am very loyal to my friends, and I want to be there for them as much as possible. Friends are people who also have illnesses, family troubles, and hardships. We need to be available to stretch out our hands to them in their need. If you don't have the time in your life now to help a friend, then maybe you are doing too much. What could you change in your life?

If friends are sick, be ready to help drive them to the doctor or pick up something for them at the store. Keep a meal frozen in your freezer so you will have one to give away quickly if a friend is in need. Be willing to babysit their children.

Be available to talk to them when they need you, in person or by phone. Try to stop what you are doing and be sure to listen well. Many times all a friend needs is someone to listen and to care. Have empathy—put yourself in their shoes. Offer encouragement. Don't nag or argue.

E-mail them a short message or a text so they know you care. This is a way to keep in touch without intruding or bothering them.

Accept your friends as they are. Praise their accomplishments and never be jealous of them. Be forgiving. And if you need to, don't be afraid to say you're sorry.

Always keep promises and secrets. A real friend never gossips, is discreet and confidential.

Speak words of hope, grace, and truth and demonstrate faith. A friend also prays for and with her friends and commits to prayer intercession for them.

Be there when a friend loses a loved one. Sometimes we don't know what to say when our friends are grieving. But a quick visit with a meal, visiting just to be available, sending a card or letter that shares how special their loved one was, and even remembering the birthday of the deceased are extremely helpful and loving gestures. Grieving is an ongoing process that requires continuing help and support. "Bear one another's burdens" (Galatians 6:2) is a verse we need to remember.

Friends are healthy! Having a community of friends around you will keep you healthier and will give you more joy in your life. Do all you can to cultivate friendships.

REACH OUT TO YOUR NEIGHBORS

If you're blessed, your neighbors are already your friends. For most of us, some are friends and some are not. But what a great opportunity to reach others for Christ! Your neighborhood can be your mission field. You don't have to go to some far-off country to have a mission. The harvest for bringing people to Christ is ripe all over the world. Reach out to your neighbors whenever you can. Witness by action.

If your neighbor just had an operation, take over a meal.

If your neighbors tell you they are going out of town, offer to pick up their mail for them.

If their children are alone after school, see if you can have them over some afternoons. Reach out to neighborhood children by being kind and interested in them. Often you don't know what their home life is like. Your love and caring might be the only attention they get.

Be a missionary in your neighborhood. The "fields are ripe for harvest" even if all seems well. We never know what goes on behind closed doors.

Invite your neighbors to your church or your church's special programs. Some of my friends invite the neighborhood children to our Awana program. Many of these parents don't have a church, but they begin to come when they see the enthusiasm of their children.

Look for ways to love those around you. We need to remember to show mercy, treat others fairly, speak to others truthfully, and forgive others completely—especially those who are different from us. Remember the story of the Good Samaritan in Luke 10? Jesus taught this story to illustrate that we are to help others, even when they are not like us.

However, we have to be careful as we reach out. How do we know which relationships are healthy and which are not? I read a study of Psalm 1 in which the author emphasized three types of people to avoid: the wicked, sinners, and scoffers. This psalm directs us not to seek the counsel of those whose actions are wicked, those who continue a life with habitual sin, and those who laugh at the things of God.

The psalm goes on to advise us to be committed to God's Word, to delight in the law of the Lord, and to meditate on God's Word day and night. If we faithfully guard our relationships and make the Word of God a priority, we can expect some amazing results. We will be firmly established, abundantly fruitful, and genuinely prosperous. Of course, remember that God's idea of success is different from the world's idea. But when we walk with Him, we are able to be in His will and our character will become more like Jesus, which is true success. Then the neighbors you are trying to reach out to will also see the Lord in your life and your witness will become even more evident.

There are many other people in our lives that we need to spend time with and care for. How do we know whom to help? Jesus gave us a commandment to love and support the needy in all walks of life: "Inasmuch as ye have done it unto one of the least of these my brethren, ye have done it unto me" (Matthew 25:40 KJV).

Another example given to us is the woman described in Proverbs 31 who reached out to the needy: "She opens her arms to the poor and extends her hands to the needy." In fact, the needy may be anyone anywhere who needs our help. But we need to be organized in our own lives so that we have the time and ability to help.

REACH OUT TO YOUR COMMUNITY AND CHURCH

This is the area of my life that includes my children's schools, community affairs, and our church. If you are interested in helping in one of these areas, here are some suggestions.

Find out what organizations help the poor and homeless in your area. You can help support them financially. You can also work in areas of need such as soup kitchens or daycare centers.

Volunteer at a school, whether in the classrooms, at special events, or for the PTA.

Help with clean-up programs such as "Adopt-a-Highway." Plant trees and flowers or pick up litter.

Help at your local community center. Contact your Chamber of Commerce and ask for areas that need help.

Volunteer at a nursing home or adopt a needy group. One school in our town helps a housing project for single parent families. The sixth-grade students collect household items, children's toys, diapers, and clothes for these families. They also collect money for these needs by having a fundraiser at a Wendy's restaurant. The students work during the event, clearing tables and getting drinks for the customers. Sometimes the night has a theme, such as Fifties Night. Wendy's donates part of their profits from the night to the project.

Join an organization such as the Junior League. These groups always need volunteers for their many programs focused on the poor.

Find out the needs at your local church:

- Are there single parents in the church? One of the greatest problems they face is the overwhelming amount of work to be done. Maybe your husband could help with a plumbing problem or you could type a résumé for them.

- Organize a special bulletin board at church listing people's needs, as well as people who can help. Then people will have a way of knowing and meeting specific needs.

- Help organize emergency food or rent support for people who are struggling.

- Help sort used clothing for your church's clothes closet, or stock and distribute food for the food pantry.

- Become a friend to the pastors and the staff at your church and help them whenever you can. They are under a tremendous strain every day trying to meet the never-ending needs of their congregation and community.

- Pray for your community, your schools, and your church. Ask God to help them and to help you know how you can reach out to others. Paul in Ephesians 6:18–19 asked for prayer:

And pray in the Spirit on all occasions with all kinds of prayers and requests. With this in mind, be alert and always keep on praying for all the saints. Pray also for me, that whenever I open my mouth, words may be given me so that I will fearlessly make known the mystery of the gospel. (NIV)

REACH OUT TO YOUR CITY, STATE, AND COUNTRY

Helping with the needy in a large city and state can be difficult. But most cities have soup kitchens, homeless shelters, daycare centers, or foster child programs.

When disaster strikes. If a tornado, hurricane, fire, or flood occurs, you should help in every way you can by financial donations, actually going to the scene of destruction to help, or opening your home to the displaced.

Volunteer as a guide at a museum, as a "Pink Lady" at a hospital, or as a reading mentor at a library. Volunteer your time to build homes through Habitat for Humanity or help financially.

Contact your representatives in Washington, D.C. and find out ways you can help the needy in the country. The United States of America is the strongest, richest, and freest country in the world. One important way we all can help is to remember to pray for our country and our governing officials. In fact, Paul exhorts us to pray for them in 1 Timothy 2:1–2:

> First of all, then, I urge that entreaties and prayers, petitions and thanksgivings, be made on behalf of all men, for kings and all who are in authority, so that we may lead a tranquil and quiet life in all godliness and dignity.

Be sure to vote! Your vote can make a difference. What you believe in and how you want your officials to make decisions are shown when you vote. Sometimes people quit voting, believing one vote doesn't make a difference. But one vote can make a difference. In 1960 John F. Kennedy won (and Richard Nixon lost) the presidential election by a margin of less than one vote per precinct nationwide. The same slight margin of votes also decided the presidential election of 2000 between Republican candidate George W. Bush and Democratic candidate Al Gore. Bush narrowly won the election with 271 electoral votes to Gore's 266.

Write letters and voice your opinions. Make your voice heard in every level of your government. As the old saying goes, "The only thing it takes for evil to win is for good people to do nothing."

Support organizations who believe as you do and are working to help preserve our freedoms. Many Christian organizations work tirelessly for our country's youth and families. Focus on the Family in Colorado Springs, Colorado, is one example of an organization that strives to protect the rights and freedoms of families. Passage of legislation that would have been devastating to families was stopped because Focus on the Family worked hard to inform people. Some of us feel it's too hard to keep up with politics and too uncomfortable to think about all the evil going on in our country. However, we need to be just as compassionate and forceful about our freedoms as our forefathers were who died for those freedoms and for us.

REACH OUT TO OUR WORLD

We Christian women need to recognize that there are many poor people in this world. In biblical times, the poor were more obvious. The Proverbs 31 woman passed the poor daily as she walked to the market. Today, most of the world's poor are located in our cities and in developing countries. We must do whatever we can to help them. As Christ said, the poor will always be with us. But we can make the choice to extend our hand to the poor. Our schedules should never be so busy that we cannot stop and be there for others.

As God causes you to feel a burden for others, don't allow the tremendous need to overwhelm you. Instead, pray for wisdom and begin with one small step. Each of us has a different circle of influence and individual ability to help those around us. If each one of us does our small part, however, needy people will be helped.

Many times the plight of the impoverished does overwhelm me. Have you ever shut off a newscast in mid-program because the world's problems were too much for you to bear that day? I am forced once again to realize I can't possibly do everything I want for others and my family. In order to do all I can I must be organized—even to the point of categorizing people by my priorities. This concept may sound cold, but it is not; it simply means my family comes first, then others. There are hundreds of organizations and thousands of people already reaching out whom you can support.

Human trafficking is real. Today there are more people enslaved than at any other time in history. It is estimated that more than *27 million people are held in slavery* and the average age of a victim is 12 years old. War, abduction, poverty, natural disasters, and immigrant labor fuel it, and global profits are estimated to exceed $32 billion dollars a year. We need to pray for these people and see how we can help, pray that God will rescue them and pray for those working to help stop this evil: "Rescue the poor and helpless; deliver them from the grasp of evil people" (Psalm 82:4 NLT).

Support missionaries from your church with finances, gifts, and prayers.

Research mission trips from your church or community. You may want to give financially to these mission areas or go on a short-term trip yourself. I was blessed to go on one with Amazon Outreach, a mission ministry to the people along the Amazon River. Before I got involved, I didn't even know this mission existed! And there are many others where we could help.

Check out organizations that provide aid to the world's poor and give to them. The Red Cross, World Vision, Billy Graham Relief, and the CBN 700 Club are only a few of the organizations who send tremendous aid to millions of people.

Adopt a child. Ministries like World Vision or Compassion International are available to support children in different countries all over the world with your small, monthly fee. Our family supports one child in Africa, and my teenager, with some of her youth group friends, helps support another. Today we can help people struggling with poverty, one child at a time.

If you think just one person cannot make a difference, think about the lifelong ministry of one woman, Mother Teresa. She began her ministry in 1948 by lifting up one dying man and helping him. Sixty years later, her missionaries operate in over one hundred countries, with about 4,000 members. Each year, the charity feeds 500,000 families, teaches over 40,000 slum children, treats almost 100,000 leprosy patients, operates AIDS shelters, homes for abandoned children, houses for recovering alcoholics, shelters for abused women and the destitute, and conducts disaster relief in some of the most unlikely places in the world.

God knows we can make a difference in other people's lives. He gave us the example of Proverbs 31:20 to encourage us to reach out to others, beginning with our own families and extending into the world. Remember that when Christ was on the earth, He didn't heal everyone or take poverty away. He did the work God sent Him here to do, just as we can only do what God has for us. Pray and ask God to show you where He wants you to help.

Bringing home Step 4

*She extends her hand to the poor; and she
stretches out her hands to the needy.*

PROVERBS 31:20

For Further Reflection

1. How can you reach out and show the love of God to the "neighbors" in your life?

2. What types of ministries does your church have, and how could you help with them?

3. What organizations do you know of that help the needy in your area? Which ones would you want to work with?

4. What are some ways you could reach out to your community, city, state, and world?

5. What are some ways your children could reach out to others?

Personal Application

One of the hardest decisions for a woman is how much time she can devote to others when she is pushed to the edge with just the demands of her own family. And I understand this so well. That's why we need to remember that God gives us seasons in our lives for a reason.

If you just had a baby, this is your season to say no to the outside world as you take care of this infant and heal yourself. When your children are in grade school and higher, you will have time to show them the many needs in their community where they can help. Prayerfully select a need with them so it can be a family activity. I don't know a better way to teach our children to care for others.

As your children enter their teen years, you may have more time to devote to your community needs. And as you become an empty nester, you will enter the season when you will probably have much more time to help.

We all need to be lights to others in this world. Just remember to ask God to show you where He wants you to reach out in every season of life.

A WOMAN WHO WANTS TO BECOME MORE ORGANIZED ...

Understands Time and Its Importance

Therefore be careful how you walk, not as unwise men, but as wise, making the most of your time, because the days are evil.

EPHESIANS 5:15-16

As we have seen in the first four steps, we can become more organized women by prioritizing our most important relationships. I believe the next step is understanding how to use time to our advantage. Good time management is crucial to being more organized. When we use time correctly, we will be able to maintain these relationships as well as accomplish what God wants for us in the many different seasons of our lives.

We all have the same 24 hours. And for busy women—and who isn't busy these days?—daily life is a constant negotiation between what needs to be done and the time available to do it. That means you and I are always on the lookout for shortcuts and time-saving strategies, but often those don't go far enough. We wind up stressed out and disheartened, feeling as if time manages *us*.

Research shows that solving problems like procrastination or chronic lateness is not just about learning some new tips; it's about recognizing and adapting to your individual nature. We need to learn about our temperaments, our energy levels, and the patterns of our life that may show us the areas of time management that we need to work on.

The one big problem is that modern life is bursting with distractions—Facebook, text-messaging, iPad games, myriad cable TV channels, Twitter, and more—that make it tough to focus on the tasks at hand. Temptations are everywhere, which rob us of the precious commodity: time. But don't get disheartened! Time management is something that can be learned. The first step is *choosing* to change and to use the time we are given each day more productively.

One thought that might help you each day is that the newness of a new day is a gift worth celebrating. Perhaps this concept was what prompted the psalmist to declare, "This is the day the LORD has made; let us rejoice and be glad in it" (Psalm 118:24). I have a tendency to become overwhelmed and so I become disheartened. God's Word is such a shot in the arm! When you become discouraged with all you have to do, get in His Word and play some praise songs. I promise that you will get your drive back!

Of course, we face many unknowns today—and some may be difficult. But the treasure of each brand-new day is so special that Moses was led to write, "Teach us to number our days, that we may gain a heart of wisdom" (Psalm 90:12 NIV). Every new day is a precious gift and God wants us to use every second whether we are working or resting in His will.

All my close friends know that early morning is not my best time of the day. In fact, I will do almost anything I can to keep from waking up early! I remember the best part of nursing a baby was not having to get up to make breakfast! But I believe God does not want us sleeping in while our children get their own breakfasts and leave for school. Of course, there are always exceptions, such as illness, but God shows us in the Proverbs passage that running a household takes great sacrifice: "She rises also while it is still night and gives food to her household and portions to her maidens" (Proverbs 31:15).

People in biblical times kept one small lamp burning through the night. In fact, for a Palestinian peasant, a lamp was considered the one expense that was a necessity. When the sun set, the door of the house was shut and the lamp was lit. Since the lamp held only a small amount of oil, someone had to wake up during the night and add more oil to keep the lamp burning. The wife assumed this responsibility so her family could sleep. Then she would stay up and begin preparing for the day. She also set the example for her servants. Since she worked so hard, they could do nothing less. She demonstrated leadership and set a strong example for her children. She believed she was "working as for the Lord" (Colossians 3:23 NIV). One of the customs of that ancient time was to cease working and close up shops from noon to three each day. The women were probably getting enough rest during this time so they were able to "rise while it was still night."

In our time, the most sought-after but elusive goal is to have "time for everything." Ephesians 5:15–16 has been called the Bible's key to time management: "Therefore be careful how you walk, not as unwise men but as wise, making the most of your time, because the days are evil" (NIV). This can also be translated as "making the most of every opportunity." It suggests an attitude toward living that sees every situation as the perfect occasion to do God's will and influence others for Him. During these evil days, we are to live out the goodness God has placed in us through faith in Christ.

How much time do we have today? Time for prayer? Time to answer a child's question? Time to be interrupted by someone in need? Time to consider others during an inconvenience or delay? Time to call or write someone who needs to hear from us? We

need to ask the Lord to give us wisdom to grasp today's opportunities, "making the most of [our] time" for what's important to
Him and our families.

Our culture is so fast-paced that few of us take the time to
actually consider where we're going. I know you don't want to
finish your life and find out you were on a course other than
God's, fighting the wrong fight, and struggling to keep the faith.
I believe God wants us to live *intentionally*—that is, the choices
we make in life have a purpose and a direct end. Ruth, from the
book of Ruth, made a definite choice to follow her mother-in-law
back to Israel, knowing full well she might never marry again. She
gave up the gods of her family and instead chose the God of her
deceased husband and his family. I believe that the Holy Spirit
gave her a spirit of truth, for her decision didn't make sense to
the world of her day. But she set her mind on this path, faithfully
following her mother-in-law, and God blessed her obedience by
providing a husband and son for her.

To keep going from morning to evening caring for children
and a household, you need more than just pure energy. A woman
has to feel called and motivated by God to please both God and
her family if she is to succeed. The following tips can help motivate you as you take another step toward becoming a more organized woman.

SET GOALS

To manage time, we need to plan our days, our weeks, our months
and our years. Think and pray about what goals you have for your
life and what you feel God's will is for your life. Don't compare
yourself with others because God has a different plan for each
person on this earth.

I understand how difficult setting and planning goals may
be for some of you. Please don't let this section sabotage you!

Some people are planners and some aren't. If you are one of the latter, just plan one main objective for your day tomorrow. As you begin to see success, you will be able to set more goals in different areas of your life. I do know, without a doubt, that setting goals is crucial to having organized lives.

List goals. Studies show that the success rate for people who write down their goals is about *ninety* times greater than for those who don't. Take time right now to do this. Start with what you want to accomplish each day, each week, each month and for the current year. These goals could be in different categories:

- Housework

- Career work

- Activities with your husband

- Activities with your children

- Personal goals for yourself

If writing down goals is difficult for you, begin with a daily to-do list. Write down each thing you need and want to do for tomorrow, and then list them according to your priorities. Going to the grocery store might be more important than finding new wallpaper, so place it at the top of the list. Just checking off each item feels motivating.

Set annual goals for yourself—and your family. Every January, our family sits down and writes out our goals for that year in four categories: spiritual, intellectual, and physical for each individual, plus our family goals. I keep these goals posted by my desk. When I review them throughout the year, I'm encouraged to try to accomplish them.

Set five-year goals for yourself. These are goals for larger projects: writing a book, saving up for a special vacation, getting your child ready for college. Many companies, at the end of each fiscal

year, write goals they'd like to see their organization achieve over
the next several years.

Set long-term family goals. Families can do the same thing to
give their lives more direction. Asking your children where they
see themselves in five years helps them to plan ahead and to realize that what they do today can affect their future.

Along with setting goals, seek purpose. In *The Purpose-Driven
Life,* Rick Warren says,

> People who don't know their purpose try to do too much—
> and that causes stress, fatigue and conflict. It's impossible to
> do everything people want you to do. You have just enough
> time to do God's will. If you can't get it all done, it means
> you're trying to do more than God intended for you to do.

I know I have this problem. I am constantly "doing." I have to
really rein myself in to stop and focus on what God wants to say
to me. If I don't, stress and fatigue make it hard to wake up in the
morning. I am beginning to learn that God asks us to do much
less than what we think we should do! And what He asks us to
do is much more important, and *eternally meaningful*, than what
we have on our to-do list.

I do know that if you are too busy for the *basics*—quiet time
with the Lord; a healthy dinner on the table for your family; time
for your husband, children, family, and friends; keeping up with
the household chores; and being a good employee—then you are
doing too much.

SET UP A COMMAND POST

Treat your homemaking job like any other professional occupation.
You are the COO (Chief Operating Officer) of your household.

It is imperative that you have your own "office" in which to
run the household, whether it's a built-in desk, a store-bought

one, or even a card table. And now that so many of us use computers, it is vital to have a dedicated place for your computer
work. If you don't have room for a desk, buy a rolling cart where
you can put your computer, folders, and desk accessories. You can
then roll it anywhere in the house you want to work.

*On your desk keep accessories just for you: transparent adhe-
sive tape, scissors, ruler, note paper, your stationery.* Don't allow
your children to use these items or they will end up lost. They
need to learn to respect your desk and its contents.

*Have a special place on your desk for a list of phone calls you
need to make.* Keep pen and paper out at all times for taking messages from your house or cell phone. Making a list of calls to be
made keeps me from feeling overwhelmed. I know if I can't get
to these calls today, they'll still be there tomorrow, listed so I
won't forget.

Keep your list of contacts up to date. When recording names,
street and e-mail addresses, and phone numbers, use a pencil, not
a pen, so you can erase and revise easily. Those of you who only
use your cell phone or computer for these records should make
changes as you receive them and, of course, make sure to save them.

Keep your desk as neat as you can. You won't lose important
papers or phone numbers if your desk is organized. Purchase a file
cabinet, folders, and hanging files if you have the funds and space
to do so, or put folders in a small stand or box. Folders are excellent for organizing important papers, receipts, bills, and children's
activities. In fact, folders are one of the best organizational items
I have. They help keep my papers in order and my desk neat. And
now folders come in so many pretty colors and styles! Other important items to have for your desk are ziplock bags to store cables
and chargers for your electronics, batteries, pens, and so forth.

Use a scanner and electronic storage. I love paper, but I can
deal with a lot less of it when I use a scanner and store it.

Dropbox and Evernote are helpful digital tools. Dropbox
lets you access documents from anywhere as long as you have

Internet access. Evernote helps you capture ideas as well as images and sounds.

Use apps. Digitize your to-dos with Astrid, an easy-to-use app that lets you prioritize and share tasks, assign jobs to friends and family, and sync your lists among multiple mobile and desktop devices (Free; Android and iOS).

Organize your papers. People ask me for help in this area every time I give a talk. Papers just seem to pile up everywhere. Separate the stacks into categories and have files, bins, and labels at the ready. Keep bills up to date as well as other important papers in their own space so you can find them easily.

- If you use the same desk for your household bills as well as your home-based business, be careful to keep them separate.

- The best way to pay bills is online electronically. Visit your bank and have them show you how to sign up for this. You will never have to use checks and stamps again! You can also check into your credit or debit cards to keep track of your spending. If your bank doesn't offer electronic bill-pay, try a program like Bluebird by American Express, which offers a virtually free way to manage your money. Create subaccounts for the kids (with daily spending limits) and use the accompanying app to track your cash. You can even pick up Bluebird cards at Walmart.

Have a calendar close by, either on your desk, in your purse, or in your phone, and check it daily. I keep my calendar open in the middle of my desk to review often. I know that many people like to keep their calendar on their phones, but I like to see the full week and month quickly. Also, the whole family can keep up with everyone's schedule. All the family's activities are written on this calendar, as well as birthdays, anniversaries, and special notes. Some families prefer a large, magnetic calendar they can put on the side of the refrigerator or wall. Each child's activities are written in a different color pen. This is a great way for the whole family to keep in touch with everyone's plans.

- On Sunday night, review the next week. Circle in red doctor appointments or anything else that must not be forgotten for that week.

- Check to see if there are birthdays or anniversaries listed on your calendar for the next week (or month, if that is easier). Add these names to your grocery list so you can pick up cards or presents.

- Every December, with red ink, fill in next year's calendar with important dates such as birthdays and anniversaries. This way, you will never forget someone special. To make sure you have cards for those birthdays and special occasions, buy all the cards you'll need for the whole year and keep them in a certain place for use when needed.

ESTABLISH A DAILY ROUTINE

Whenever I am asked what the most important tip is for being more organized, my answer is to plan. Each day has just a few windows of opportunity for getting different tasks completed. I know that if I don't get the house clean on cleaning day, there just isn't another time slot for it.

So along with planning, it's vitally important that you establish daily routines to help you stay organized. One of my favorite routines is my famous "five-minute quick clean" routine morning and night.

Keeping a house looking nice doesn't need to take hours and hours; five to thirty minutes can do wonders. I have a two-story house, so I straighten the downstairs (the living areas) at night before I go to bed, and the upstairs (the sleeping areas) before I leave for the day. The goal is to keep your home picked up, clutter eliminated, and dirty clothes and trash in their correct places. If you have young children, plan which household task is important to do each day and have your children help with it. Make a game of it; they'll have fun and help you too. (*See more in Step 9.*)

Keep similar items in their own "zones." When you keep household and hobby items in their own places, you won't lose them. For example, try putting all your sewing items in one area of the house, all the children's toys in their own area, etc.

Try to finish your tasks early in the day. This way you'll have more free time for your own projects and activities.

Schedule a stay-at-home day every week. I choose Mondays because it helps me organize my week. I like to change the linens on my bed, get the house clean, do the laundry, and I usually cook a complete dinner. However, sometimes this home-day changes because of doctor appointments or activities so we have to be flexible! Another idea that might help you is to get your family to help you clean. Sometimes we all would take an hour and pull together: my husband would vacuum, the girls would dust and change their beds, and I would mop the kitchen and start the laundry. Having their help was such a time saver for me. Plus, the children are learning that being part of family is helping with the home as well as practicing life skills.

Schedule a "playing" day. I like Fridays. When the children were small, this is the day I would take them to the park, to the mall, or to a friend's house to play. Now that my children are older, I use this day to shop or have lunch with a friend, play tennis, or just read. Even if I only have a few hours, I try to do something I really want to do.

Try to do chores before the weekend so you are free to be with your family. Saturdays should be for fun, not work. Of course, large projects like finishing the basement or getting the yard ready for spring may have to be done on weekends, and those of you who work outside the home during the week will probably need to do your chores on the weekend. Schedule a set time when the whole family can work together on these projects, and the rest of your weekend will be free.

Set up traditions to help you schedule your week better. Our children liked to have pizza every Friday night. I liked it, too. It was one night I didn't have to cook. We also have traditions for holidays, which I find helpful when it comes to planning.

MAKE THE MOST OF YOUR TIME

Scheduling our days and keeping up with our goals are difficult tasks. The biggest problem for most of us is simply finding enough time. Here are some tips.

Reduce your choices and prioritize. In our busy lifestyles, there are too many choices to make, from which activity to be part of to which running shoes or fat-free salad dressing to buy. Sit down and determine the most important areas in your life. Then simplify and set priorities.

- Prioritize commitments. A good friend shared with me that at one time in her life she was involved in almost every club in her small town, besides helping at church and her children's school. After prioritizing, she decided to concentrate on just two areas of volunteering: her church and her children's school. In this way, she could give herself more fully to the Lord and to her family.

- Simplify your purchases. Buy just the amount of make-up or clothes or household items you need. Yes, that Strawberry Liquid Face and Body Gel looks pretty, but do you really need it in your life? Maybe just a good, healthy soap can do the trick, reducing your costs and freeing space in your bathroom. I try to make buying choices based on what will keep my life as simple and as carefree as possible. "Stuff" brings more responsibility.

Get rid of everything you don't need. I have gone into every area of my house, throwing out what we no longer use and cleaning out the cabinets, drawers, and closets. (*See Step 9 for details.*)

Learn to say no. For some of us, this is the hardest rule. We women are taught to do for others. I personally want to help everyone who calls me. But if I say yes to everything, I am actually being selfish to my family. Since most activities people ask us to do are good things, our decision to help comes back to our personal goals and priorities. That is why it is vital to have these already decided. If a request lines up with your goals and priorities, you can say yes. If it doesn't, you can say no and not feel you have let someone down. Being in balance and following God's will invites freedom. Remember that though there are many *good* things we can do, God only wants us to do the *best one* rather than a bunch of good things.

Find your energy time and use this time for your hardest tasks and projects. When my children were little, my worst time of the day was when I put them down for their naps. I would just collapse, then feel guilty that I wasn't using this free time for chores. Finally I realized I'm a night person. Night is when I have the most energy. I began to nap when the children did. Then as soon as I put them to bed at night, I had several hours to work with no interruptions. I used this time to clean house, do laundry, iron, pay bills, and sew. Of course, I was able to work at night because my husband traveled. When he was home, I adjusted to his schedule. If your husband doesn't travel or if you are a morning person, then obviously nights won't work for you. What is important is that you find your own energy time.

Don't be afraid to delegate. This is a hard area for me because I think I can do it all. I forget to ask for help. My husband reminded me that the less I do the more opportunities he has to help. This really opened my eyes. I realized I was doing a disservice to my whole family by not involving them in the running of the household.

- Assign chores to your children. Find a chart to hang in the kitchen and let your children choose the chores they want (make sure they are age-appropriate). My children preferred me doing it all—at first. But now that they are on their own, they have a sense of pride that they know how to clean and cook and are able to take care of themselves. One of the best ways to give your children self-confidence and a good self-image is by giving them chores. (*For more tips about assigning chores, see Step 10.*)

- With your husband, write plans or lists of ways he could help you. If you sit down with him and talk about your needs, he will be willing to help. Mothers of preschoolers especially need their husband's help.

- Find a friend, neighbor, or other family member you can ask for help. This is especially important for single mothers.

- Review the chores you do that take too much of your time and find a better way to do them. I've decided I don't have time to wash my car, so I pay the extra few dollars when I fill my car with gas and let the machine wash it.

- Hire a teenager. We used to pay a teenager in our neighborhood to mow the grass, which was a great help for us as well as helping him. This freed Saturdays for family time and helped this young man earn some money. If you enjoy washing the car and mowing the lawn, look at other time stealers in your routine and see if someone else can do them.

Time yourself. Set a time limit and race against the clock. Try to get your morning chores finished before lunchtime. If you accomplish that, reward yourself with a walk, a long phone call to a special friend, or a start on that extra project you have wanted to do.

Don't let your tasks expand to fill the time. Set the time and shorten the time for the task. You are the one in control of your day and the goals you want to accomplish. If you were working in an office and your boss said you could leave two hours early if all your work was done, most likely you'd work much faster than normal so you could leave. You can make this principle work at home, too. Recently, I set 9:00 PM as my goal to be finished with everything I need to do each night. This is a hard goal. At night, I usually wander around watching the news on television, making phone calls, and catching up on my laundry. Before I realize it, it's late and I haven't sat down to read, which is what I've been waiting all day to do. Now I try to get the little things finished, the cats put away, and the lights turned out by 9:00 so I can go upstairs and have time just for me. I even told my children that after 9:00, I will not help with homework or sign papers. This might seem harsh, but it makes them stay on task and become responsible for their own time management.

Realize how much time can be wasted on the computer. Time management specialists even recommend that you only check your e-mail at set times each day. If you aren't disciplined in this area, set a timer while you are checking your e-mail, logging onto Facebook, etc., to help you stay on task.

Stop procrastinating! Everyone, including myself, has times when they just can't do what they should do. For example, I knew I had a writing project to finish, but there was always something else crying for my attention. Finally, I stopped paying attention to those things and concentrated on what I knew had to be done.

- If what you are putting off seems an overwhelming task, break it up into manageable steps. Clean one room at a time instead of trying to do the whole house. Sometimes, the dread of a task is more stressful than the task itself. For example, we decided to finish our basement, which meant we had to move everything stored there upstairs. I didn't think we could do it. But once we just started, it wasn't nearly as bad as I had thought it would be.

- Just do it! Begin on what needs immediate attention. For example, if you know you have to write thank-you notes, get the stationery out of the box and onto your desk. Perhaps address the envelopes. Then, when you are at your desk waiting on hold, start writing those notes.

- Focus on what is important about whatever you are putting off. If, for example, you can't seem to get your thank-you notes written, focus on who they are for: special people in your life. Wanting them to feel your appreciation should be enough motivation to get on with the task at hand. This is how I tackle my struggle with cooking. I would procrastinate cooking dinner if I could. But I focus on keeping my family happy and healthy, not how tired I am at cooking time.

- Plan a special reward for yourself when your task is finished. Think of something you really like to do. Promise yourself you can do it as soon as you finish your task.

- Tell yourself you can't do something else you want to do until you have started on this goal. If my goal for the day is to plan the holiday party for my daughter's school, I put off my walk or phone calls I want to make until I reach that goal. Sometimes you must discipline yourself to do what you *should* do rather than what you *want* to do.

We must live every area of our lives with discipline and with a purpose for the Lord.

> Therefore, since we are surrounded by such a great cloud of witnesses, let us throw off everything that hinders and the sin that so easily entangles. And let us run with perseverance the race marked out for us. (Hebrews 12:1 NIV)

HAVE A PLACE FOR EVERYTHING

This is important if we want to keep our homes streamlined and organized. Plan a place for the daily newspaper and put it there as soon as you're finished with it. Keep all your tools in their proper place and teach your children to respect your property by doing the same. If you can't decide where something should be stored, place it where you think it will be used the most. Another great reason for having a place for everything is that you won't spend precious time searching for items you can't find. I hate to lose things, so I am very motivated to keep everything in its place.

If you think your family could never learn this principle, think about how a preschool or kindergarten class operates: Children are playing all over the room with every toy imaginable when suddenly, the teacher blows the whistle and says, "Story time in two minutes!" Immediately, each child knows where to place his or her toy and in two minutes, the room is back to normal!

Put things away. You will save hours of cleaning time plus hours of searching time if everyone remembers to put things away when they are finished with them.

Establish a set place for everything. Go through every area of your house and straighten and organize to decide where each item belongs. Always put the same things in the same places:

- receipts in your wallet

- tickets to upcoming events in a special place on your desk or wallet

- mail in a pre-determined inbox with perhaps different levels for each family member's mail; you might also want to go to CatalogChoice.org, which helps you control catalogs and unsolicited mail you receive in your mailbox

- magazines and catalogs where they won't clutter

- newspapers in a tidy stack and recyclables in a special bin

- car keys, sunglasses, scissors placed in a special area or basket each time you are finished with them

Be ready to throw things away! The average person handles about three hundred items of paper a day (bills, mail, magazines, etc.). If you can't think of a use for an item now, toss it out.

Hold a family meeting. Let each person know where things now belong in the home. Ask for their help. No one can keep a home organized without each family member's help.

As you come across items you don't want, set them aside in one area of your basement or garage. We call this area our "garage sale" area. When it gets full, we have the garage sale! This is also a great time to give away outgrown toys or items to someone who can use them.

HANDLE PAPER ONLY ONCE

Have a set routine each day for when you will read the paper and dispose of it and when you will get the mail and dispose of it. When sorting mail, separate into five stacks:

To do. This stack is where I put papers or mail that needs a response, like an invitation to a party that requires an RSVP, a letter I need to answer, or a thank-you note I need to write immediately. I have a special place on my desk for this stack. Some of you might prefer to use a basket to keep these in one place.

    I also make stacks for my husband's and children's mail. I put my husband's mail on his desk and my children's mail at their place on the kitchen table. When they came home from school, they immediately saw their mail when they got their snacks. Once my children went to college, I would place their mail on their desks in their rooms or send it to them. Also, I never opened their mail.

To pay. This stack is for all the bills. I also stack here anything from my children's school that needs a check, such as an upcoming field trip. I have one section on my desk for bills to be paid on the first of the month and another section for bills needing to be paid later in the month.

To file. Put your receipts, insurance forms, or recipes and decorating ideas from a magazine in this stack. If you have room for a file cabinet next to your desk at home, file these immediately or place them in a bin or basket to be filed later.

To read. Isn't it great to have something to read when you're waiting in line or in a doctor's office? You might want to have a basket where you place articles, magazines, or books that you want to read. You can just grab what you want to read and take it with you.

I have a table next to my side of the sofa where I keep all my magazines. I try to keep this current. As soon as I finish a magazine, I give it away, throw it away or save it. (Since decorating is one of my passions, I can't throw away my decorator's magazine for a while!) I keep bookmarks in the magazines I'm reading so when I have a few minutes, I can pick up where I left off. When I see an article I like, I pull it out to make sure I won't forget to read it or file it.

To toss. Finally we come to the main stack: your wastebasket! Most of the mail that we receive is junk. Don't let it clutter up your life. Make a quick decision, recycle what you can, and throw away the rest.

Just remember, you can save yourself hours every week by being organized with your mail and paperwork. However, I know this is an area of stress for many of you. When I speak, there are always many questions about how to organize all the paper and mail that come into a household. I hope these ideas help.

PUT GOD FIRST

This is one hint you probably haven't seen in many time management classes: our Lord has to be first in every area of our lives for us to be successful. It is His will we are to follow every day. We must ask ourselves, "What am I doing with my life and with my time that will last forever?"

Becoming organized women should not be the main focus in our lives. We should want to be more organized so that we have more *time* to give to the Lord and His work. His Word and His people are the only things that will last forever.

Before setting goals and writing to-do lists, we first need to pray about what God wants for us. Planning our days based on God's priorities provides a much greater sense of peace and purpose than anything we could schedule.

> *Commit your works to the LORD,*
> *And your plans will be established.*
> **PROVERBS 16:3**

Bringing home Step 5

There is an appointed time for everything. And
there is a time for every event under heaven.
ECCLESIASTES 3:1

For Further Reflection

1. How do you begin each day? What time do you usually go to bed and get up in the morning? Do you like your daily routine?

2. How can you make the most of your time? Do you have time stealers in your routine?

3. What type of organizational tools, like baskets or bins, do you use to keep things in their place?

4. What routines would you like to have scheduled in your life?

5. Do you find time every day for your most important priorities?

6. Do you have time every day with God?

Personal Application

Review how you spend your days, weeks, months, and years. What could you change in your schedule to make the most of your time and life? As you begin to review your schedule, walk around your house and see if there are changes you can make to your desk (command center); where you handle the mail; and if items have special places so they won't get lost. Are you procrastinating in any one area, and have you set goals? Proper time management is very important in helping you become more organized.

A WOMAN WHO WANTS TO BECOME MORE ORGANIZED ...

Balances the Demands of Her Home and Career

Well done, good and faithful servant.

MATTHEW 25:23 NIV

Balancing home and work can be very difficult. Women are pulled in so many directions today. The expectations placed on women now far exceed those from any other time in our history. There are so many talented, educated young women today, many more than when I went to college. Where are they going to invest their talents and time? Should they continue with their education? Where can they find meaningful work? Should they stop or interrupt their careers to raise a family?

The answers to these questions will be different for each person, so only you can answer these questions for yourself. But the main place to look for the answers is in God's Word. The verse above helps to narrow the field of questions. Whatever we choose to do with our lives, may we be doing God's will and may He be the one pleased. Pleasing God with the work of our lives is the ultimate litmus test.

Proverbs 31 shows a woman, married, with children, who still works in many different areas. I believe that working outside the home is not a bad thing. But I also believe that shifting our priorities from the right ones to the wrong ones is. The woman in these verses is creative, industrious, and provides for her family:

> She considers a field and buys it;
> From her earnings she plants a vineyard. . . .
> She makes linen garments and sells them,
> And supplies belts to the tradesmen. (Proverbs 31:16, 24)

And there are other women in the Bible who worked. We read in Acts 16 about Lydia, a businesswoman dealing in textiles, who was the first convert to Christianity in Europe. She had an eye for design and a flair for making money. Imagine the passion and drive it took for a woman to succeed in business in the ancient world! She was obviously successful since she owned her own home and it was large enough to become part of her ministry. Whether Lydia had children is not revealed, but we do know that God gave her incredible gifts. I believe that as the Spirit flows in you, God will lead you to develop and share your own gifts just as He led Lydia.

When my mother was raising her first three children, she didn't even have a car. Most families had just one car, and that was for the husband to use for work. She didn't have the health clubs, commitments, jobs, or weekly women's meetings that we women have in our life today. She took care of her family and home and she loved every minute of it, probably because she didn't have other things pulling her in different directions.

Today women are bombarded with opportunities and pressures to have a career, to "be somebody." If you are single, or a single mom, staying home is probably not an option. You are likely the sole support of yourself or your family.

If you are married and your husband is able to support the family, you still have some tough choices to make. I personally have a hard time when mothers who don't need to work do so for extra material comforts. As unpopular as this perspective might be, I feel compelled to say mothers have to put their children's best interests before their own. If that means a career has to be put on hold or the old car needs to be driven another few years, so be it. Children are not acquisitions. They are precious human beings who need a parent guiding them every day. A day care center, used every day, will never offer them the care, instruction, security, and love that a parent can.

I know women who chose to work full time but carefully interviewed and hired a caretaker who would come to their home. Their children were able to keep to a schedule in their own home. If you have to work, this is a great alternative to day care.

If you are struggling with this, sit down and review exactly how much money you will bring home after deducting child-care expenses, new work clothes, dry cleaning, gas and parking, lunches and taxes. I have talked to many women who realized they were making only a small income after these were deducted. These moms have pointed out they would save money, with fewer doctor bills, if their preschoolers were home more. They would also spend less on take-out food and money spent to relieve stress.

If you are undecided about whether to work or not, read books on how it might impact your preschoolers. Burton L. White wrote a book entitled *The First Three Years of Life*. In it, he gives evidence that the first three years are vital to a child's development. He recommends waiting to go back to work until your child is at least three.

What can we learn from the Proverbs woman? She "considers a field and buys it; from her earnings she plants a vineyard" (31:16). This wife is also an entrepreneur, a "working woman." She wants to increase the wealth of her family and is always on the lookout for things she can do. She first thinks through her purchases and then buys from her own earnings; her husband doesn't give her the money. She has learned how to save. But what type of "job" is this? She is working to help her family and the work is probably right in her own backyard. In other words, the field is probably next to her house, so she really has a "home-based" job!

Through the years, I have had many part-time jobs (part time because I simply could not leave my children in day care). I was fortunate that my husband could provide for our family, but we were also prudent in our spending. We didn't have furniture in the living room and dining room for eight years. I took full advantage of this, though, because I turned the dining room into a playroom. Since it was adjacent to the kitchen, I could keep an eye on my children all the time. After breakfast, they would play in their playroom until nap time or errand time. There was no television in the room, so they didn't ask to watch it. Only in the afternoons after their nap did they watch *Mr. Rogers' Neighborhood* or *Sesame Street* in the family room.

Even though people might have laughed at us because our home wasn't completely furnished, our children benefited. And that was what was important to me.

Our society today is very different from the time of Proverbs and biblical women. According to the Bureau of Labor Statistics, 70.6 percent of mothers with children under the age of 18 work outside the home (2011) compared to 28 percent in 1960; 64.2 percent of women with infants to kindergarten age now work. The Working Mother Research Institute surveyed more than 3,700 women to find out who stays at home, who goes back to work, and some of the factors that shape those decisions. They found that even in this day and age, women have problems with these decisions. At-home moms, for example, are more likely to say they feel frowned on by society than working moms, while working moms are far more likely to say they feel guiltier about the condition of their home than about spending too much time at work. Working mothers do carry a greater burden of guilt and feeling judged by their at-home counterparts, but the gap has become surprisingly smaller. As I read this report, I again felt the need to remind all of us not to judge others. Some of you have to work; some of you want to stay at home. We must trust that each woman decides what is best for herself and her family.

However, the actions we take and decisions we make in life ultimately lead to specific outcomes. Some of these outcomes we can anticipate, and others simply blindside us. One brave divorced mother decided to share her very personal, poignant, and heartfelt story in the book, *Secret Regrets: What if You Had a Second Chance?* Here is what she said about being a working mom:

> If I had a second chance, I would have quit my job when my children were born. I would have not made so many excuses to say, "I have to work." Because they were mostly lies. Lies told, because honestly, the weeks I did spend at home scared me to death. It was easier to hire someone to mother them, and pay her to do my job.

The wife of one of my church's pastors told a different story. She has always worked full time, even when her children were infants. They were able to find a friend who wanted to be a nanny. This young woman helped raise their children. The outcome? This family works together so beautifully that everything gets done, in harmony. The wife loves her work. The husband truly is part of his family. He does the laundry, picks the boys up from school, and participates with dinner. Each boy is responsible for his room, toys, homework, etc.

I share these stories to show that even the most dedicated mothers have to make hard choices, and that solutions to problems may not come the way you expect. My prayer is that you won't feel guilty with whatever you choose as long as you are asking God to show you His will.

The issue is how to balance everything together. This is why I believe there are different seasons in our lives. Some seasons are to raise children and other seasons are for other types of work.

If you are a single mother, or a woman who must help your husband bring in enough money for the basics, being organized is crucial. You are the precious woman who has so little time to do it all. To keep an outside job, the housekeeping responsibilities, and raise children, any woman has to be highly organized.

Here are some tips that may help you.

FIND THE RIGHT JOB FOR YOU

Find a job you enjoy that uses your talents. Theodore Roosevelt said, "Far and away the best prize that life has to offer is the chance to work hard at a work worth doing."

How do you find a career you love or create passion within yourself for the job you currently have? One way is to find "work worth doing" as Roosevelt said. Evaluate your skills, your strengths, and your talents and explore how they might translate into a career that provides opportunities to help others. For example, a photographer could give her time to take photos of animals for adoption at the local humane society; restaurant work could lead to donating food to a shelter; a teacher could volunteer to tutor in the afternoons at a Boys and Girls Club or shelter. As you evaluate your current skills, make sure to research online courses or a local community college where you could learn new skills.

While you are looking for a job that's right for you, begin to form good habits that will help you be more successful. Whether your full-time job is being a single woman, a mother, or an employee, there are some habits that effective people incorporate in every area of their lives.

Stephen R. Covey wrote a book called *The 7 Habits of Highly Effective People.* The 7 habits are:

1. Be proactive

2. Begin with the end in mind

3. Put first things first

4. Think "win-win"

5. Seek first to understand, then to be understood

6. Synergize

7. Sharpen the saw; that is, undergo frequent self-renewal

If you have very young children but you need to work, first look at options other than full-time work. You will not make as much money working part time as you would full time, but the few years at home invested in your children will reap tremendous rewards.

Consider something you can do at home. Look into book-keeping or secretarial services, or sell goods or services from your home. Beauty companies such as Avon, Mary Kay, or Nu Skin are examples of home-based businesses that have made many women successful from their homes. If beauty's not your interest, there are a wide variety of other businesses to choose from: try nutritional food supplement companies such as ReLiv, or kitchen aids such as Pampered Chef or Tupperware. Selling jewelry is another business that has started in the last few years. Stella & Dot and Premier Jewelry are brands that have done very well. If you have an entrepreneurial spirit, start your own business. Women are earning money from home selling their own crafts or fashions, performing desktop publishing or graphic design, telemarketing, researching via the Internet, and more. The need for money does not automatically have to drive you out of your house. The rising use of the Internet and telecommuting by fax, Skype, and e-mail make this the best era in decades for earning money from home.

Consider working in a hospital. I have friends who can work one or two twelve-hour nights a week while their small children sleep. The income from this is equivalent to working a full week. Some of you, like myself, might not be able to work all night without sleeping, but this is another option to consider.

Consider working at a church. Churches often have part-time positions available, either as a secretary or working in the nursery on Sunday mornings. Many churches hold a preschool during the week. This is an excellent option for mothers of preschoolers. They can bring their children to the school while they work.

Consider working at a school. Once their children are in school, many women become teacher's aides or teachers themselves. They can be home with their children in the afternoons and during school breaks.

If you are already working full time, look into a part-time position for the same company or ask about a job-sharing position. Many companies are eager to keep a good employee and will try to arrange hours that work for you.

If your job requires traveling, look for ways to make the schedule work for your family. I speak at workshops, seminars, and retreats. When my daughters were home, I tried to schedule overnight retreats no more than once a month. Weekly seminars were scheduled so that I could be home in the afternoon. I also kept some days free for housecleaning and cooking. I always wished I could lead more seminars, but at that time in my life I couldn't. If your boss is requiring too much travel, talk to him or her about this. Your boss may not be aware of your particular situation.

KEEP A RIGHT ATTITUDE

Be excited about the journey of life! It's easy to start thinking everything is too hard, or that there's just too much to do. This is a mistake I make too often. If you feel life is too hard, ask yourself, "What is missing? What is wrong?" Ask God to help you refocus on the life He has given you and to find joy. Remember that what we *do,* more than anything we *say,* reveals what we truly value the most.

When you are at work don't feel guilty about not being home, and when you are at home don't feel guilty about not being at work. Leave office problems at the office so you will be available 100 percent to your family when you are home. Keep your life as balanced as you possibly can.

In your job, remember to please yourself too. Don't take on extra work just to please someone else. Set limits on how much you'll be available to others at work. Set a time when you know you need to be home with your family and stick to it.

Keep a daily to-do list and include at least one thing that you want to do, even if it's reading a magazine for five minutes. Have something on your list that will be enriching, restorative to your spirits, or simply fun. This is important to your emotional well-being.

Write a family mission statement. Ask your family what the most important thing to do together is. For one family, it might be eating dinner together every night. Another might want to have a family night once a week. This will help you to treat your family as more important than your business.

Remember who you are really working for. "Whatever you do, work at it with all your heart, as working for the Lord, not for human masters" (Colossians 3:23 NIV).

BE REALISTIC IN YOUR DAILY GOALS

Remember, you can't do it all. Break the pattern of doing too much. Recognize your limitations. Try delegating more and asking for help, which is simply sensible management, not weakness. Think of yourself as the organizer of your day. Plan when you can do certain tasks so you won't be overwhelmed when it's time to go home.

Balance your tasks between priorities and demands. I define *priorities* as something important to you that you want to do, while *demands* are something important to someone else that you feel you should do. Doing only what you want is selfish, while doing only what others want is unendurable. Each day should contain both.

Understand the value of a simple daily priority list. This list will keep you aware of what's really important and help you stay away from the unimportant.

Then, don't forget to make lists. Make grocery lists, Christmas present lists, things-to-do-today lists.

Put urgent items at the top of the list. If you run out of time or energy before you've finished the list, those tasks will have been accomplished.

If you have a home-based job, keep it physically separate from the rest of the house. Work in a closed-off area or room, with your own desk, phone, and other supplies. This will help you keep your home life and work life separate. Warning: If you run your home business from your bedroom, the visual reminder of the work piled up will prevent you from truly relaxing when you need privacy or sleep. If possible, use the basement or spare room instead.

MAXIMIZE YOUR TIME

If you work full time, hire outside help to keep up your house, and use more convenient foods or eat out. You need extra time for your family. You should not try to be a super woman and do everything. That leads to a stressed-out mom who is no fun to be around.

Maximize your time by scheduling. If you are unable to afford hiring someone to help clean your house, schedule a day (or evening) every week when you can get the basics done, such as vacuuming and laundry. You won't worry then about how clean your home is the rest of the week.

Maximize your time by delegating. Each member of the family should contribute to the upkeep of the house and their own rooms and clothes. We are our children's teachers, not slaves. Delegate chores to each family member and set a time for each to be done. This will instill responsibility in your children as well as prepare them for their future when they are on their own.

Use your lunch time for errands, exercising, or personal phone calls so you will have more time at home. (Remember to pack a lunch so you still eat something.)

Be smart when you use the telephone. Make notes about what you will need to discuss before you place a call. Keep the discussion brief and to the point. Always be polite and cordial, but stay on the subject. Try timing each call, ending the conversation when the set time is up. Leave detailed messages on answering machines so others can respond with an answer more quickly.

Be smart when you use the computer. Check e-mails only at certain times of the day, and time yourself when you are on Facebook or other social media so you don't waste time.

And be smart when using your phone to text or play games. I feel that one of the worst problems in our country is people of all ages whose heads are bent over their phones all day long. Discipline yourself to turn off your phone during the day and evening. Do not go to sleep with your phone next to you.

Avoid long lines, traffic, and other time wasters by living off-peak. Go to restaurants early, do your grocery shopping late at night or early in the morning, and buy Christmas gifts all year long.

When a holiday or special event is coming, do as much as you can early. I try to have everything finished for Christmas by December 1. This way I have time to enjoy the season and go to parties and school and church functions for my children without the stress of trying to get ready for Christmas (see my book: *12 Steps to Having a More Organized Christmas and Holiday Season*).

Be aware that saving money can cost time for yourself or your family. A buffet dinner for $4.99 sounds great, but if you have to stand in a long line and waste a lot of time, the $6.99 dinner across the street would really be cheaper. Your time is worth something.

Use every service you can afford to help you save time and energy. Three good examples: automatic deposit for your paycheck, automatic payment for your utility bills or mortgage, and paying your bills online. Other services that can help you are the different apps for your phone as well as many websites. And one program that might be a lifesaver is called LastPass. It stores all your passwords in one place, so all you need to remember is the password to your LastPass account! It's free and available as a computer program or a mobile app.

Let your family know when they can and can't interrupt you. It is vital for all family members to understand the importance of your job and that distractions can hurt your productivity. This step will help you avoid getting caught in the crossfire of competing demands from your boss and your children.

Identify the hardest part of your day or the most stressful thing you do and change it if you can. When it is taken from your schedule or modified, you'll be able to do so much more. For example, don't try to cook dinner on your busiest or longest day. It is hard to walk in the house at six and then try to put a meal on the table. Put something in the slow cooker that morning before you leave for the day or let that be the night you eat out. Your day will go more smoothly if you take some stress out of it.

Remember, when you make a task easier, you don't just save time, you make your life better. "Dost thou love life?" Benjamin Franklin once said. "Then do not squander time, for that's the stuff life is made of."

Realize that if you work, you will have to be highly organized to get everything done at home. But also realize that you will have to be flexible. When things aren't going well, *you* are still okay! Our Lord can help us through anything and will give us the strength to accomplish everything we have to do.

HOW TECHNOLOGY CAN HELP

When this book first came out twelve years ago, so much of the technology that we have today wasn't even invented! Today, technology can help you balance your career and home.

Pay your bills online. This one step has saved me hours, plus lots of postage expenses! If you don't know how to set up your accounts, a representative from your bank can help you.

Use e-mail for everyday communications. By sending out e-mails you can save yourself time that would have been spent on the phone. Most appointments come via e-mail now, as do social activities. So keep these up to date and use e-mail as often as you can. Also, instead of jotting down phone numbers, ask people to digitally send their contact info to your phone or e-mail.

Text more. I know seeing everyone's head bent down over a tiny phone is irritating, but texting has improved my life! Now I can keep up with my children and family faster because phone calls take so much more time.

Keep your inbox up to date. Keep on top of your e-mails and get rid of spam. Make sure your spam blockers are on, or set your inbox security to the highest level. For e-mails you don't want to receive anymore, reply with "Unsubscribe" in the subject line, or click on the "Unsubscribe" button at the bottom. Some of you may want to have two e-mail accounts. I have one that contains my most important e-mails and another that I give out to stores, restaurants, etc.

Use electronic schedules and to-do lists. For those of you who have a very busy schedule it may be best to keep all of your appointments and to-do list electronically. Find a calendar program and to-do list that you like to use and keep it up to date. Internet-based programs such as Google Calendar allow you to share calendars with your family so everyone is in the know. This is also a way to keep up with birthdays, doctor appointments, and reminder notes to yourself.

Set up a photo sharing site for your family. This is also known as storing your pictures "in the cloud." Sites like Shutterfly.com, SmugMug.com, Flickr.com, or Facebook.com allow you to store all of your photos online. You can add events like birthdays, holidays and family get-togethers and have everyone post their pictures for the event. You can add notes about the occasion so that years later you can look back and remember what took place. And you can protect your privacy by authorizing who gets to see the pictures. Storing photos on the Internet is very secure and protects your files from getting lost if your computer crashes.

Teach your kids proper web etiquette to protect them. Whether they're using Facebook or any other popular social network, kids should be taught that there are important safeguards to follow. Teach your kids these simple rules: never post rude or derogatory comments, improper photographs, or where they are going. Never share your location with anyone other than your friends, and don't post your travel plans where anyone can see them. You should also follow these rules and monitor your children's online activity.

Use apps. There are so many apps now that can help with everything from finding great recipes to making chore lists. Here are some you may like:

- Kroger Co. This one is amazing. You can load coupons onto your Kroger Card so that it automatically deducts them along with your Kroger Plus discounts. No need to carry coupons anymore. Go to the Kroger site, create an account, associate your card with your account, and there you go.

- Motivated Moms is a great app for organizing your household chores.

- AllRecipes.com Dinner Spinner and Epicurious Recipes and Shopping List: both of these apps help you find recipes.

- Color Splash is a must-have for those of you who like photo editing.

- 2Do is an electronic version of your to-do list.

- Cozi Family Organizer is a free app and online shared calendar with to-do lists, a shopping list, and a family journal.

YOU'VE GOT MAIL!—
UNDERSTAND HOW TO USE E-MAIL EFFECTIVELY

Part of being more organized is understanding where you are disorganized. I have a feeling that most of us would never think that our e-mail is a problem—but we might be wrong. We are now in information overload with over *2.9 million e-mails* being sent every second around the world!

In the not-too-distant past, when you wanted to set up a meeting, ask for help and advice, or simply share something with someone, you would pick up the phone, send a letter, or meet face to face. These took some planning and effort. But today, communication is friction-free. You can send a message from anywhere in the world at any time of day. You can even use a smartphone as a computer that can be with you 24/7.

When I talk with business professionals as well as moms, I hear constantly that e-mails are a huge task on their to-do list each day. Yes, sending e-mails can help with your workload, but when it takes hours to go through them each day, it can cause some serious problems. Here are some ideas to think about before you hit "Send":

- Respect recipients' time. Only send e-mails that are really important.

- Brief is good. It's OK if replies aren't long. They need to stay on point. Keep yours simple.

- Be clear. Clearly state what your subject is in the subject line. And make sure you change this when the subject changes. Many times this is how others can locate an e-mail.

- Be careful you who CC. Only send a copy to someone else if it is mandatory that they have one.

- Attachments. Only use one when it must be used. Otherwise, keep the information in the body of the e-mail.

- Thank you. Once someone says "thank you," don't reply again with an added "thank you."

WORK PRODUCTIVELY

There are many proverbs written on the benefits of hard work. Here are two to remember:

Lazy people are soon poor; hard workers get rich (Proverbs 10:4 NLT).

Work hard and become a leader; be lazy and become a slave (Proverbs 12:24 NLT).

Think back to stories you remember hearing from your grandmother's and grandfather's early lives. They worked hard! If they were farmers, their day began before sunrise and lasted way after sundown. Today, many complain when asked to work hard. I would love to see my grandparents' work ethic instilled back into our culture. Billy Graham's book *Just as I Am* gives a great example of this. He shares about his early life working hard on his family's dairy farm:

I learned to obey without questioning. Lying, cheating, stealing, and property destruction were foreign to me. I was taught that laziness was one of the worst evils, and that there was dignity and honor in labor. I could abandon myself enthusiastically to milking the cows, cleaning out the latrines, and shoveling manure, not because they were pleasant jobs, certainly, but because sweaty labor held its own satisfaction.

Think about the kinds of tremendously hard work most women had to do in the past. Household helps such as washing machines, vacuum cleaners, indoor plumbing and water have just become available in the last hundred years. Before that, women had to do everything by hand. In biblical times, a woman like the one described in Proverbs 31 was responsible for grinding the grain each morning, which often required half a day to complete. She had to do the cooking, weave the cloth, and make clothes for her family. She had to take care of the flocks that provided the wool for cloth, and she was also responsible for caring for the goats. Washing clothes took a great amount of time, because she had to go to the nearest source of water and dip and beat the clothes with a club. The women were also the ones who had to go to the well or spring for the household water and water for the animals. They carried pitchers of water on their head, shoulders, or hips. This was heavy and time-consuming work.

And, of course, she had to take care of her babies and children, and manage the upkeep and cleaning of the home. I don't know if I would have survived back in those days! These women never had to drive carpools or go to PTA meetings, but they faced illness, death, and starvation on a regular basis. Let us look at our workloads with thankfulness for all the modern helps we have.

Begin to view your work at home and outside the home as important. As our attitudes change toward the positive, we will have more energy and desire to work hard at whatever we have to do.

Try to always have at least one enjoyable home project or personal project. This will help keep you motivated, because you will finish what has to be done faster to get to what you *want* to do. The old saying is true: "If you want something done, ask a busy person." The more we have to do, the more we are able to get done. Of course, having too much to do can have the opposite effect and keep you from getting anything done at all. Balance is the key here. Think of the things you have always wanted to do or make but never thought you had the time or talents for. Narrow this list down to one thing and do it.

Do your chores first thing every day. Part of working hard is starting the day productively. You will never get behind because you will be using your energy on what has to be done. Then you will have time to do what you would like to do.

EXPRESS YOUR CREATIVITY

Hard work is important, but you also need to *enjoy* the life you live. That is where creativity comes in. The Proverbs woman "works with her hands in delight" (Proverbs 31:13). How can you make your daily homemaking job more fulfilling and enjoyable? How can you imbue work outside the home with real purpose in your life?

Start with your attitude. View your life and the work you do in it as a gift from God. "Whatever you do, work at it with all your heart, as working for the Lord, not for human masters, since you know that you will receive an inheritance from the Lord as a reward. It is the Lord Christ you are serving" (Colossians 3:23–24 NIV).

Review your passions. Try to identify your gifts and talents. What are your passions and interests? Could you find another job that suits you better? Could you work differently around the house so that you have more joy in the work?

Look at your jobs and responsibilities in a new way. Use your creativity to turn any difficult chore into a special memory.

Do you have to visit your sick grandmother in the nursing home? Take a game for you two to play or take her outside for a picnic or a walk. Do you need to clean out the garage? Turn a difficult chore into a fun learning time by asking your younger child to count everything the two of you take out of the garage. Do you dislike going to the grocery store? Plan to stop at your favorite deli when you're done shopping and pick up a great sandwich as a reward.

Plan one day a week or one event a week that you can look forward to. Having something to anticipate can really be motivating and can help keep your spirits up. Being creative can add a special dimension to life. I bring this even closer by having one thing a day I can look forward to! When the girls were little, I knew that sometime each afternoon I could sit down with a snack. I would go over the mail at this time and when they were in school, I would sit with them and talk about their day. Another thing I looked forward to was taking a walk each day, even if only for fifteen minutes.

Rethink what you want to do with your life. Make a list of everything you wish to accomplish or experience. Include your dreams.

- What hobbies would you like to pursue?

- What new things would you like to experience or try?

- What do you find really fun? What makes you happy?

- What have you been putting off that you would feel better about if you completed? Or started?

- Would you want to study again? How about art, a new language, or a cooking class?

- What could you do to be more creative with your health, body, level of fitness and sense of well-being?

Be creative with your future. What things have you done in the past that have brought you joy and meaning in your life? How can you continue them into the future?

Be creative with your emotions. Quit allowing your negative emotions to get the better of you, and show positive and joyful emotions to your family and to yourself. Did you wake up in a bad mood? Make up your mind to change the bad mood and be happy to see your family. On a rainy day, find one thing that's sunny and concentrate on it. Allow yourself to love and to be loved.

Ask yourself how you could be more creative in each area of your life: in your home, in your relationships, and in your personal life. This might seem a little overwhelming, but part of becoming a more organized woman is thinking of ways to improve every area of your life. Ask God to help you in this process.

Consider a craft project or adding something beautiful to your home. Take a look at one of the many magazines that offer ideas on how to be creative in your home, your yard, and your kitchen. *Martha Stewart's Living, Good Housekeeping, Real Simple,* or home decorating magazines are some examples. There are also many craft and hobby shops (such as Hobby Lobby and Michael's) that can give you ideas. Many of these stores also have classes you can take to learn a new craft. Walk through your home with paper and pen and write down ideas about how to organize each room or how you can creatively make it into your home.

- Make a wreath with silk flowers to go over your fireplace, or put together a vase of dried flowers for the hallway. Another idea is to make decorations for your front door that match whatever season you're in. I have four different arrangements for our front door and I love changing them as the seasons change.

- Make scrapbooks using paper items or create one online. My daughter has created some beautiful photo albums using digital photos. Visit Snapfish.com for digital photo printing, free online photo sharing, and unlimited storage.

- If sewing is a way you want to express your creativity, make curtains for the kitchen or drapes for the living room.

- If you don't have the money or time for a large sewing project, make and furnish a small dollhouse for your daughter. You will be teaching her to be creative and to use her talents while having fun yourself.

- Make a quilt. I always wanted to do this, but never thought I could do an entire quilt. But I've discovered a sewing store where I can buy one square a month, beginning in January and ending in December. After I finish making the last square, I'll have enough for one quilt! Remember, a quilt can make a lovely wall hanging too.

- Hand-sew cross-stitching and make beautiful pictures or verses that could be framed for your home or for presents.

- Begin a collection of some kind and showcase it. I have a friend who began collecting tea cups some years ago. Because many of us knew about her collection, she often received a tea cup for birthdays, anniversaries, and Christmas. Each cup is different. My friend had a lighted cabinet made to display this beautiful and unique collection. Other people collect antiques, dolls, or miniatures. There are many choices about what to collect, which is what makes this particular project so expressive.

- Use plants to express your creativity. Plants can easily change an ordinary room into a warm and inviting one. Visit a local nursery and talk to the staff. They'll have wonderful ideas about the type of plants that would work best in your home and for your climate. (Philodendron is one species that works well anywhere and is hard to kill!)

Every one of us can be creative, even if we don't think we can be. There are hundreds of possibilities for making our homes more beautiful and personal. This is one of the results of becoming a more organized woman. As our lives become more organized and balanced, we are able to go to the next step: making our lives more beautiful.

Ask God to give you the strength to work hard and the ability to be creative in every area of your life. Focus on the beautiful instead of the mundane, and you'll move from existing to really living!

> *Every skilled woman spun with her hands and brought what she had spun—blue, purple or scarlet yarn or fine linen. And all the women who were willing and had the skill spun the goat hair....Then Moses said ... "See, the LORD ... has filled him with the spirit of God, with wisdom, with understanding, with knowledge and with all kinds of skills."*
>
> **EXODUS 35:25-26, 30-31**

Bringing home Step 6

She considers a field and buys it;
From her earnings she plants a vineyard.
She makes linen garments and sells them,
And supplies belts to the tradesmen.

PROVERBS 31:16, 24

Today, more women are working outside the home. Balancing a career and home life is more of a challenge than ever. Each woman will have to decide what works best for her. My suggestion? Place your prayers before God and let His Holy Spirit find the right solution for you and your family.

For Further Reflection

1. What are some ways you could bring in extra money without having to sacrifice time with your family?

2. Can you think of other tips for balancing a woman's home life and her work life?

3. What was the Proverbs woman's main motivation for working?

4. If you are exhausted from working full time, what could you change in your life to reduce your workload?

5. In what areas of your life could you change from being somewhat lazy to being more hardworking?

6. How important do you feel your attitude is as you go about your household chores? Do you "work with your hands in delight"?

7. Remember that you can't do it all. What are the most important things you should do each day?

Personal Application

Take time to reflect on how your work schedule (home schedule as well as your job schedule) affects you and your family. Do you feel that any changes need to take place, or are you satisfied with how things are? Discuss with your family any feelings you have, positive or negative, so that they can support and help you. Also, go through your home, either mentally or physically, and ask yourself, "How could I work harder or more efficiently? How could I use creative ideas in my home to make it a haven for myself and my family?"

A WOMAN WHO WANTS TO BECOME MORE ORGANIZED . . .

Stays Healthy and Fit

She girds herself with strength
And makes her arms strong.

PROVERBS 31:17

We may be the most organized women in the world, but if we lose our health we won't be able to do anything at all. My grandmother understood this principle very well. Her own mother became an invalid at a young age and she experienced the hardships and trauma of seeing her unable to live a full life. She often reminded me to do all I could to stay healthy because "without your health you just can't do anything."

Fortunately, our culture is beginning to lean toward healthier lifestyles. The organic farming sector grew by 8 percent in 2010, which is a very large change from regular farming methods. Today, there are many individual gardens being planted, restaurants are serving healthy foods, and even some staple grocery items like cereal are being formulated with unprocessed ingredients such as whole grains.

However, the majority of people who end up in the OR are overweight or obese and many have type 2 diabetes. Forty percent of Americans are obese and 50 percent of Americans are on daily medication due to dietary issues. These are staggering statistics. The U.S. Department of Health and Human Services estimates that $117 *billion* is spent each year on treating diseases that are rooted in obesity.

Diabetes has become an epidemic. There are now nearly 26 million diabetics in this country; and at least one in five girls and one in four boys born in the year 2000 will be diagnosed with diabetes in their lifetime. Type 2 diabetics are up to four times as likely to die from heart disease. It's estimated that women diagnosed by the time they're 40 will lose 14 years, on average, from their lives; men, almost 12.

Most Americans today consume 156 pounds of sugar a year versus 18 pounds in 1880. This huge difference is making our insulin levels go haywire. We used to grow our own food, but now most of the food we buy from grocery stores contains over 40 varieties of sugar. I highly recommend reading product labels when you shop. If sugar is one of the first three ingredients, don't buy it.

But there is a source of hope: A study published in the *New England Journal of Medicine* determined that more than 90 percent of type 2 diabetes cases can be prevented by lifestyle changes. The disease is often triggered by poor diet and inactivity, because fat interferes with the body's ability to use insulin, the hormone that carries glucose from our bloodstream into our cells. Patients can completely rewrite their fate by losing weight, eating the right foods, and getting in shape. To make this change, we must have a whole new philosophy and mind-set. We can't just diet and exercise. We must change how we look at food and at our bodies and make lifelong changes.

There are four areas to concentrate on to stay strong: exercising, eating proper food, dealing with stress, and getting enough rest. As you begin to incorporate these principles into your life, you will step closer to being a more organized woman.

MOVE YOUR BODY EVERY DAY

You must move your body every day for energy and for optimum health. In fact, a recent report states that sitting down all day is one of the worst things we can do for our health. If you sit in an office chair or on your couch for more than six hours a day, your risk of heart disease increases by up to 64 percent. That's like shaving off seven years of your life! You are also more at risk for certain types of cancer. Simply put, sitting all day may be killing you. However, there are two ways to counteract this problem. Remember to stand once an hour and get about 30 minutes of activity per day, which can be split into three sections of 10 minutes each.

Next, find some form of exercise (moving) that you enjoy and set goals for yourself.

- Write down why you want to exercise. Tape your overall goal to your refrigerator or desk where you will see it often.

- Write out a plan of how you will reach this goal. My plan is to walk every day and work out with light weights. You may want to put your walking shoes out by the door to remind you to walk.

- Be realistic with your goals. It takes time to get in shape, to get stronger, and to lose pounds.

Ease into exercise. Don't start a sport or activity without gently warming up your muscles, and stretch off and on during the day. You can even stretch while watching TV.

Pick something that is fun. That's why I walk. I really do love it. It can be used as a time to think, pray, and plan as well as a time to be with others. Walk with your husband at night after dinner. Think of all the uninterrupted time you can have with him. Or, walk with your teenager. This can be a great opportunity to spend one-on-one time with him or her.

Look for activities you can enjoy throughout the year—skiing in the winter, tennis and swimming in the summer. Find activities that make your life full, enriching, and alive.

If you have the time and desire, go to a fitness class, or sign up for tennis, golf or swimming. The rewards of a healthier you are worth the time and effort these may take.

Use your muscles to keep your whole body strong. If you are unable to get outside to exercise, use the stairs in your house: run up and down them. Or exercise to a workout video. Every bit of exercise helps. Even bending down to get something out of a low cabinet, or doing leg lifts while on the telephone helps keep you in shape.

Get your heart rate up. As you begin to exercise, work on increasing your heart rate. Aim to reach 50 to 85 percent of your maximum heart rate (the number 220 minus your age) for at least 30 minutes, five days a week.

Remember to stretch! It will improve your flexibility but it also makes you stronger. All you need is seven to ten minutes every morning when you get out of bed. This is actually one of my motivations to make my bed. I start my stretching as I reach for the blankets and pillows and then I finish stretching and do some yoga.

Lift weights. Weight training can help increase your joints' range of motion, especially in older people.

Practice yoga. I used to think that yoga or Pilates didn't do anything for the body. Was I ever wrong! These are excellent activities to build the strength of your core muscles as well as your arms. Studies also show that yoga increases the rate at which glucose moves from the blood into our cells, which will help manage or prevent Type 2 diabetes. It also reduces levels of stress hormones, which can cause an accumulation of abdominal fat.

Stand like a stork! Keeping your balance strong can help keep yourself safe during a workout, but balance decreases with age. To improve and maintain your balance, stand on one foot while you brush your teeth. For added benefit, stand with your eyes closed.

Jump rope. This exercise is fun and easy—plus, it's great when traveling. It burns lots of calories and it also builds stronger bones. Jumping (even around your house if you don't use a rope) grows and strengthens leg bones.

Get fit with a friend. I have some friends who work out together in a gym and others who go to Weight Watchers together. Still others meet as a whole group every morning at the school bus stop and walk together after the children leave. They say being together really helps them to stay on course. Perhaps find a walking buddy at work and you can walk during lunch or breaks.

Get fit with an app. Perfect for exercise newbies, Couch-to-5K provides detailed 20-30 minute running and walking routines, which slowly ramp up in intensity and frequency ($1.99 on Android and iOS).

Phone it in. Multiple studies have found that high-tech gadgets—such as pedometers, activity-gauging armbands, and fitness apps—help people stick to exercise programs.

Find the right time of day for you to exercise. My husband works out at 6:30 a.m. I could never do that, but that is the best time for him. Once you have picked out the best time for you, stick with it. Once you have exercised for three weeks, it will become a habit.

Interval training. One of the best ways to get the most from your workout is to alternate intense bursts of activity with short periods of easier activity. One example would be to do a walk/run each day where you walk for a few minutes and then you run for a few minutes.

Go outside! Studies have shown that there are incredible physiological benefits of being outdoors, including increased immune activity and less perceived effort during exercise. Being outdoors also helps to dispel depression and improve our attitude toward exercise. And though we have to be careful to use sunscreen, the vitamin D that we get from the sun is beneficial.

Find time each day to breathe. Yes, I know you know how to breathe! But by purposefully breathing the right way a few times a day, you will be able to restore your body and feel better. When you are at a stoplight, in the carpool lane, or waiting in line, take a deep breath and count to six. Then, very slowly let the air out, also counting to six. Do this for one minute. You will be amazed how much better you feel!

Pamper yourself. Our bodies do get tired and rundown, so we need to focus on them as we restore ourselves. I know those of you with tiny babies or a full-time workload have a hard time finding a way to pamper yourself. If you're in this situation, try some of these suggestions: take a 10-minute walk around your office building or neighborhood; go outside and look at the flowers, trees and clouds; take a bubble bath; read a magazine or book; clean out your makeup drawer and buy something new; get a massage or a facial; go out to lunch or dinner with a friend; visit some shops you never seem to get time to see.

I know exercising to get in shape can be hard for some people. But I have found that if I do even a little exercise, I really do have more energy. I realized this in a new way during a blizzard. We couldn't go anywhere because we were snowed in. I had so much fun reading, watching TV, playing with the girls, and just being lazy. But by the third day, I didn't feel I had the energy to brush my teeth! I realized the less I do the less energy I have. The next time I'm stuck at home, I'm getting on my treadmill—no excuses!

EAT PROPERLY EVERY DAY FOR ENERGY

Food is the fuel our bodies need, and making the right food choices will help keep us going. Keep in mind that exercise alone leads to a very modest reduction in total body weight: less than 3 percent! To achieve effective weight loss, you have to pair exercise with the right diet plan.

What's the number one reason Americans are heavy? The brain, very smartly, wants nutrition. But the average American is eating empty calories. So if you eat 2,000 calories but they are mainly junk food, your brain says, "Keep going until you get nutrients." We need to remember to eat the right foods every day for our health and for better energy.

For some people, losing weight or keeping weight off is almost impossible. I don't mean to minimize that hardship, so I suggest going to a weight-loss professional who could work with you if weight is a substantial problem. The main way to lose weight is by eating less and exercising more, but your body weight can be the sum of many physical and psychological hardships. The following tips are just some basic helps.

Dieting isn't necessary; just concentrate on eating the right foods at the right times in the right amounts:

Stay away from fatty foods and eat plenty of fruits, vegetables, and grains.

Avoid the white groups: white flour, white bread, white rice, and potatoes.

Especially, stay away from processed food. Try to eat food straight from the farm or farmer's market.

Read labels. The first five ingredients on a label explain what the majority of the food contains. Anything ending in "ose" is added sugar, and anything ending in "ol" is sugar alcohol, which can be just as fattening.

Try eating four or five small meals a day instead of one or two larger meals.

Use an app to help manage your diet. Tracking calories is simple with Lose It!, winner of the Surgeon General's Healthy Apps Challenge. Tap foods with the barcode scanner and the app automatically deducts the calories from your daily budget. It's free from Android and iOS.

Plan when you will eat. If you are on the go most of the time, the only food available is what you find on the road. So plan ahead and pack a small ice chest or tote bag with snacks or a lunch. You will eat much healthier as well as saving money and time!

Track what you eat. It is easy to munch mindlessly throughout the day. People who track what they eat can lose twice as much weight as those who don't, one study showed. You can use a notebook or one of these websites and apps: PeerTrainer.com; the app Lose It! (see above); DailyBurn.com; and SparkPeople.com.

Eat protein. This one type of food does many things. It promotes healthy skin, hair, nails, bones, and muscle. It's also a fabulous weight loss aid, according to a 2005 study from Arizona State University. It helps control hunger by making us feel full and satisfied, and it helps to burn calories. Beans, nuts, steak, eggs, poultry, and fish are great choices.

Never skip meals. Your body will try to compensate by holding on to the food already there.

And never skip breakfast. Not eating breakfast can increase your risk for obesity more than fourfold! Eating breakfast stabilizes your metabolism and sets it for the day.

Be boring. Eating the same meal every day can be a good idea. Research shows that people who've successfully maintained at least a 30-pound weight loss for a year or more tend to consume a diet with limited variety; similar meals over and over may lead them to feel fuller faster and eat less overall.

Stop late-night eating. People who eat at night gain three and a half more pounds a year, on average, than those who don't. Both body and mind stand to benefit from an earlier meal: eating 70 minutes to two hours prior to bedtime could decrease your risk of stroke by 76 percent! One possible reason is that blood sugar, cholesterol, and circulation changes brought on by the digestive process may disrupt blood flow to the brain. Eating right before bedtime may also cause acid reflux and heartburn.

Do not eat at fast food restaurants unless you can order something healthy. It's best not to go there at all!

Pay attention to portion sizes. We have gotten used to large portions in our country, but they are one of the major reasons for our obesity problem. Here are some guidelines: a piece of chicken or other meat = size of a deck of cards; amount of breakfast cereal = ½ cup or the size of a tennis ball; amount of cheese = 3 dice; amount of peanut butter or hummus = the size of a golf ball; amount of pasta or rice = the size of a light bulb.

Use smaller plates and containers when packing a lunch. Most people don't need a full sandwich: one half is plenty along with fruit and vegetables in the lunch. Also don't buy potato chips. They add nothing to your meal nutritionally but they do add fat.

If you love chocolate or sweets, choose one kind and have a small piece to curb your sweet tooth. However, indulge in dark chocolate! It contains flavonols, the antioxidant-rich compounds found in cocoa (see below under "Eat stress soothers").

Be aware of foods that are fat releasers. *Reader's Digest* just published their new diet plan called *The Digest Diet.* The editors learned a fascinating thing: Not all calories are created equal when it comes to shedding pounds. There are 12 food groups that have a special ability to thwart your body's desire to hold on to fat, so you lose quickly and without hunger. You can go to their website, www.digestdiet.com, for menus and recipes. These items are: calcium (helps control your hunger—found in greens, yogurt, milk, and cheeses), resveratrol (found in red grapes, mulberries, and peanuts), coconut oil, unsaturated fatty acids (found in olives, olive oil, nuts and seeds, dark chocolate, and avocado) and poly-unsaturated fatty acids (found in fish and many nuts and seeds), proteins (listed above), vitamin C (deficiency in this vitamin helps the body cling to fat), quinoa, honey and cocoa, fiber and vinegar.

Be aware of high-energy foods. These are often quick and convenient, and can keep you going through a hectic day (see sidebar for suggestions from Nancy Clark's *Sports Nutrition Guidebook.* Though these were written by a nutritionist, remember to consider allergies and unique dietary concerns you may have).

Remember to drink lots of water as you're going through your day. We all need at least eight glasses every day. Water helps the condition of your skin, aids digestion, and helps you control your food intake. Carry a water bottle in your car at all times and drink from it regularly!

Drink green tea. This tea contains the highest concentration of powerful antioxidants called catechins, which lower the risk for some cancers as well as lower "bad" (LDL) cholesterol and promote weight loss.

Eat stress soothers! Four foods have been found to boost your mood and protect your body. They are fish (has essential fats that may help moderate stress hormones and protect against depression); dark chocolate (research reveals that this food can lower blood pressure and reduce stress hormones; however, eat only a few small squares a day because of the fat content); black tea (may help you recover from nerve-wracking events more quickly; it can lower the stress hormone cortisol); and avocado (this food has two powerful stress fighters—potassium and monounsaturated fatty acids—which can lower blood pressure and help ward off depression). The report even mentioned that eating crunchy foods—like celery or carrot sticks—can help relax a clenched jaw and ward off tension. (From WebMD and *Reader's Digest*.)

HIGH-ENERGY FOODS

1. **Whole grain bagels**. A great source for energy because bagels are complex carbohydrates. They are quick and easy to fix, and great to eat on the run or during those between-meal slumps.

2. **Spinach**. These greens are packed with magnesium. Most women, particularly those who endure stress or strenuous exercise, consume less than optimal levels of this mineral, says Dr. Mildred Seelig, former president of the American College of Nutrition.

3. **Beans**. This food can help with problems of low-level iron deficiencies, which cause sluggishness. They are also an excellent substitute for meat for vegetarians. A quick way to eat beans would be a bean soup.

4. **Tuna**. Sometimes called brain food, tuna contains tyrosine, an amino acid. Once digested, tyrosine helps to manufacture brain neurotransmitters that help you perform mental activities. This protein also helps keep your muscles fit and helps you recover after a workout.

5. **Strawberries**. Fruits are a wonderful source of complex carbo-hydrates. Strawberries are especially rich in vitamin C, which helps your body absorb iron.

6. **Oatmeal**. A great source of fiber. Fiber helps slow digestion so your body gets a steady stream of energy as carbohydrates gradually flow into your bloodstream. Since this happens grad-ually, eating oatmeal is much better than a candy bar, which gives a fast blast of energy followed by a quick crash. Hurried mothers like to grab something quick, but you will suffer for not eating right the first time.

7. **Low-fat yogurt**. A great source of calcium, which we need for our bones. Researchers now suggest calcium may reduce men-strual cramping and premenstrual water retention.

8. **Bananas**. A great energy snack. The sugars in bananas and other fruits are an easily digested form of carbohydrate. In addi-tion, bananas supply a heavy dose of potassium, an electrolyte that helps maintain normal muscle and nerve functions, and also helps prevent overheating.

9. **Soybean products**. Doctors believe that soybean products might cool off those menopausal hot flashes. Soy foods are also loaded with calcium, which can battle the bone loss associated with osteoporosis after menopause. Buy some soy milk and make a smoothie by blending the soy milk with a little orange juice concentrate and a sliced banana, or pour it on cereal instead of regular milk. Tofu, also a soy product, can be added to soups, stews, and casseroles, or crumbled into spaghetti sauce, soup or a salad. You can also buy crunchy toasted soybean snacks in many supermarkets or soy protein powder to mix with juice.

LEARN TO CONTROL THE STRESS IN YOUR LIFE

Sometimes it seems as though our days have two speeds: hurried and breakneck! It's never too late to learn how to control the different stresses in your life. And when you do, your body, mind, and spirit will become as one: healthy and vibrant.

Place prayer as one of your top priorities. Nothing will take stress away more than time with your heavenly Father. "Cast your cares on the LORD and he will sustain you; he will never let the righteous be shaken" (Psalm 55:22 NIV).

Listen to praise music. Along with prayer, music can really change the content of your thoughts and the stress in your life. If you're caught in traffic, waiting in line or waiting at the airport, use this time to pray and praise.

Make time your friend, not your master. Learn to say no to the unimportant and yes to the important. I know you have heard it before, but you must make time for yourself. If you don't, you'll start to suffer from chronic stress, which can wreak havoc on your mood and energy. And when you aren't doing well, all your relationships will suffer.

Learn and practice deep relaxation. Just taking a deep breath can take away some stress. Breathe in for a count of six, then release slowly for a count of six. It will totally change how you feel!

Meditate. Meditation has long been known to reduce stress as well as lower blood pressure and bad cholesterol. However, I believe that as Christians our meditation should consist of prayer and reading the Word of God. Meditate on happy things (Philippians 4:8).

Remember the importance of play. Have something in your life that is fun and set times for it in your daily schedule. "Plenty of people miss their share of happiness, not because they never found it, but because they didn't stop to enjoy it" (W. Feather).

Associate, whenever possible, with gentle people who affirm your personhood. The power of connecting with others cannot be overstated. Seek out those people who want your friendship.

It took me years to understand this. I would spend time at gatherings with people who didn't like me because I thought I could change their minds. But I discovered that being around people who undermine me causes me lots of stress. Now, I seek time with people who care for me.

This principle also works with family members who cause you stress. Be loving and giving to them, but keep your distance when you can. Family gatherings at holidays can be especially stressful. The same disagreements usually occur each time the extended family gets together. Pray and plan ahead, and avoid those topics or people who start disagreements. If you focus on those you care for the most, the holiday will end better with less stress and deeper bonds formed.

Be forgiving. Studies show that forgiveness can lower blood pressure and heart rate and reduce depression, anxiety, and anger. The Bible teaches over and over how important forgiveness is. Max Lucado says: "Forgiveness is unlocking the door to set someone free and realizing you were the prisoner!"

Spread kindness. The golden rule is golden because it is so special! Doing good things for others is one of the foundations of our Christian faith. And while you are spreading kindness, you will think less of yourself and your problems as you think and do for others.

Reduce all the clutter and unnecessary stuff in your life. Too much stuff really can add great stress to your life. Alexander Pope wrote that "order is Heaven's first law." This quotation was included in a magazine article by Gretchen Rubin, who is the Happiness Expert for *Good Housekeeping*. She writes:

> This quote shows me how surprising but inescapable the inverse relationship between happiness and clutter is. For me—as for most of us—fighting clutter is a never-ending battle; although I'd labored to clear clutter as part of my first happiness project, I wanted to find additional strategies to

stop its insidious progress. When I can finally find the things I am looking for, and I can easily fit a letter into a folder or a towel onto the shelf, I have a comforting (if illusory) sense of being more in control of my life generally. Eliminating clutter makes the burden of daily life feel lighter.

Inspired by William Morris's rousing call to "have nothing in your house that you do not know to be useful, or believe to be beautiful," I resolved to go shelf by shelf, then drawer by drawer and closet by closet, to consider each of my possessions. Did one of us use it or love it? Would we replace it if it were broken or lost? If so, was it in the right place?

I have added her quote because she so clearly explains how clutter and having too much stuff can cause stress in our lives.

Live within your means. In other words, be wise with your finances. Financial woes are the main reason for divorce in this country. There will always be those with more than you have, but there are also those with less. Learn to be content with what you have in this season of your life. "I have learned to be content whatever the circumstances" (Philippians 4:11 NIV).

Don't let any one thing dominate your life. Examples include an addiction to watching television, too much time on the computer, games on the iPad, or reading for hours on end. Balance what you like to do with what you need to do.

Free yourself from all dependencies such as addictive relationships, addictive drugs and alcohol, and obsessions of any kind. Your obsession might even be romance novels. Anything that takes you away from life, your responsibilities, and your walk with God has the power to become addictive. I also need to mention this: although pornography is usually a male problem, women are becoming addicted as well. And the new *50 Shades of Grey* series is nothing more than pornography for women.

Author and blogger Jennifer Degler writes,

It deeply saddens me to learn that millions of women and teenage girls are reading *50 Shades of Grey*. I am grieved by the number of Christian women on Facebook who describe how they couldn't put the book down and are anticipating reading the next book in the series. Simply put, if you are a Christ-follower, don't read this book. It is female erotica, meaning that it is written to entertain and turn you on sexually. It is pornography without the photographs. If you wouldn't want the men in your life to view pornography, then apply the same standard to yourself.

These books will cause you to visualize sex not with your husband but as described by the erotic material. The same process happens to men when they feed themselves a steady diet of pornographic images. They begin to crave the images more than sex with their wife.

Jennifer started reading romance novels in the fifth grade. By high school she had become bored with those and started reading more advanced, R-rated ones. As she says,

> Words create powerful images in our minds. I was never exposed to pornographic photos as a child, but that didn't matter because the mind can create more vivid images than a camera could ever capture. And I wanted to experience what I read about and imagined. Long, sad story short: my high school and college years were filled with foolish choices that I regret tremendously. It has taken me years of personal and spiritual work to untangle the mess I made in my own brain.

I have added Jennifer's comments because I truly believe many of you may be having problems with this type of addiction. Addictions cause life-endangering stress. Getting free is easier said than done. Go to someone who can help you if you are having trouble in this area. Christ came to free us: "If the Son makes you free, you will be free indeed" (John 8:36).

Guard your personal freedoms: your choice of friends, your freedom to think and believe as you do, your freedom to structure your time, your freedom to determine your own goals. By this I mean, don't let the opinions of others cause you to change your choices. I care too much about what other people think and I have to remind myself to follow God's will in my life first. (Of course, in a marriage, you should consider your spouse in these decisions, but both of you should love each other enough to allow each other these freedoms.)

Don't allow troublesome relationships and situations to drag you down. Take action: either restore them or end them. Troublesome relationships can really cause a lot of stress. I have had relationships with friends who are just plain hurtful. When I ended these, a lot of the stress in my life ended too.

Plan each day carefully, and make sure you don't create your own stress by doing too much. Find some time to be alone every day so you can pray, think, and plan. If you don't take care of yourself, you won't be able to care for anyone else.

GET THE REST YOU NEED

It really is true that our bodies need seven to nine hours of sleep every night. If you get this rest, the difference in your energy level and temperament will be remarkable. We set the emotional climate for our homes. If we are patient and understanding, our home life will reflect that. But without proper rest, we can become impatient and rude to the very people we love the most.

Life is a busy combination. It seems there are always more things to do, places to go, and people to meet. And though we want a meaningful life, a fast pace can rob us of the quietness and rest that we need.

God Himself "rested" on the seventh day. And even though He had hurt and sick people all around Him, Jesus went apart from the crowds and rested a while (Matthew 14:13; Mark 6:31). He wouldn't have been able to do His job right if He had been too tired and exhausted, and neither can we.

Psalm 131:2 is a psalm we should listen to: "I have . . . quieted my soul; like a weaned child rests against his mother, my soul is like a weaned child within me." Do you want to feel quiet and peaceful like that? Find a place to be alone. Turn off the distractions that keep you from listening to God's voice, and let Him speak to you as you read His Word and rest.

During the age of the Proverbs woman, when the heat was at its worst, there was a break of activity between noon and three o'clock. This is a wonderful example for us to follow. Try to rest sometime during the day. I get so tired and hungry in the late afternoon that I have a break when my children come home from school. I snack with them, catch up on their day, go over their papers, and review their homework while I get a rest. Besides giving me special time with my children, this break helps me to have the energy for cooking dinner.

But perhaps you are having a hard time getting a good night's sleep. After the birth of my first daughter, I had the hardest time going back to sleep after her middle of the night feeding. This was usually around 4:00 a.m., and to this day, if I wake up at night, it is right around 4:00 a.m. If you're having similar problems, these suggestions may help.

Deal with worries before you try to sleep. Write down any concerns and troubles with possible solutions and then forget them as you get ready for bed. I even write down things I want my husband to help me with and leave them on the kitchen counter. Then I know he knows the stress I am under and can get these things done.

Aim to go to bed and wake up at the same time every day. This is a healthy habit that will help set your melatonin levels. Stick to a bedtime that gives you optimum rest.

Avoid watching TV, surfing the web, or looking at your iPhone.
While computer work is constant in most of our lives, it can cause
problems with sleep. A recent study has found playing video
games, working on the computer, and even texting on a phone
before bed is not a good idea if you want a good night's sleep.
Emotional stimulation, as well as the back lighting on the screen,
can disrupt your natural melatonin levels. Reading a book and
listening to soft music are more effective bedtime activities.

Sleep helps our brain! New research shows that lack of sleep
ages the brain.

And naps are healthy! A study from California has found that
an afternoon nap increases a person's memory and ability to learn
and absorb new ideas. An additional study at the Salk Institute
also found napping benefits heart function and hormonal balance.

Avoid caffeine in the late afternoon or after dinner. This isn't
just coffee, but soda, tea, and cocoa. Caffeine is a well-known
cause of sleeplessness.

Don't use tobacco. Nicotine can cause shallow sleeping.

Have a healthful bedtime snack. Try a small glass of milk.
Studies show that people sleep better if they aren't hungry, but,
of course, don't eat a heavy meal within two hours of bedtime.

Relax. Some people work too hard at getting to sleep. Get in a
regular routine at bedtime. Perhaps a ritual of a nightly bath and
good book will prepare you for sleep.

FINAL THOUGHTS ON GETTING HEALTHY:
YOU COULD REVERSE YOUR AGING!

As I get older, and no, we can't stop aging, I am interested in
finding ways that will at least slow it down! Elizabeth Blackburn,
PhD, who won the 2009 Nobel Prize for her research on DNA and
telomeres (those protective caps on the ends of our chromosomes
that keep our genetic material safe from damage), made some

unbelievable discoveries. Every time a cell divides, the telomeres tend to get a little shorter, which makes our cells age. When telomeres get too short, cells stop working properly.

The good news is that Blackburn and one of her colleagues discovered an enzyme that replenishes and repairs frayed telomeres, helping us stay healthier as we get older. This enzyme, called telomerase, slows the rate at which telomeres degrade, and research indicates that healthy people with longer telomeres have less risk of developing the common illnesses of aging—like heart disease, diabetes, and cancer, which are the three big killers today.

They discovered some lifestyle factors that boost telomerase naturally:

- A diet high in omega-3 fatty acids. Foods rich in omega-3 include flaxseed oil, fish oil, dried chia seed, nuts, and vegetables.

- Exercise. We must exercise enough to break a sweat. Exercise mitigates the effects of stress, which can shorten telomeres.

- Stress reduction. Try incorporating stress reduction techniques like prayer into your life.

Keeping a healthy lifestyle will insure that you and I are healthy enough to do God's will in whatever He has chosen for us.

> *Therefore I urge you, brethren, by the mercies of God, to present your bodies a living and holy sacrifice, acceptable to God.*
> **ROMANS 12:1**

Bringing home Step 7

*Beloved, I pray that in all respects you may prosper
and be in good health, just as your soul prospers.*

3 JOHN 2

We must be healthy and have tremendous energy in order to accomplish everything in our day. It is important to stay fit so we can achieve our daily goals and live the life that God has for us.

For Further Reflection

1. Think about how often you exercise. If you feel you don't have time to exercise, what are some activities you could do instead?

2. What foods help you to have energy? Is there a time during the day when you like to eat? How could you use this time to make yourself healthier?

3. What causes you the most stress in your life? What could you do to relieve some of it?

4. Are you getting enough rest at night? Are you able to nap or take a short break during the day? If not, how could you add rest to your schedule?

5. What could you add or subtract from your life to make yourself healthier?

6. Do you have a project you keep putting off? When could you begin this project? (Perhaps you will need to work late once a week to finish it.)

Personal Application

Review how you exercise, how you eat, and how you rest. What could you do differently? Let your answer reflect the best "you" for your family.

A WOMAN WHO WANTS TO BECOME MORE ORGANIZED . . .

Works to Provide Healthy Meals

She is like merchant ships;
She brings her food from afar.

PROVERBS 31:14

You might remember pictures of old sailing ships from your history books. Ships were once the primary means of transporting goods between countries. However, sailing them was dangerous because of many problems including unexpected storms. Comparing the Proverbs 31 woman to one of these ships is a high compliment because it reveals that she will do almost anything and go almost anywhere to obtain food for her family.

Feeding a family requires a great deal of effort and energy. I grew up in a family of seven children, and many of my childhood memories are of my mom cooking in the kitchen. She always made us birthday dinners (anything we requested!) and birthday cakes. In the South where we lived it was the custom to cook big meals every night. It wasn't until I became a mother that I fully realized how hard that was. Unfortunately, most people don't cook real meals for their families anymore. And sometimes just dialing the pizza delivery number seems like a hardship! Perhaps we need to reevaluate our job description as the cook for the family. How can we show our families we love them by our cooking? What meals can we cook that won't take all day but will be tasty and nutritious?

Food is such an important part of our lives. From the moment a baby cries out her first breath, she is ready to nurse. Food becomes not only a way to keep our bodies alive, but also a source of comfort and love. Every holiday and special occasion is usually centered around food. Food is used to feed our bodies, but food also has a deep and lasting emotional purpose in our lives.

Because of this, the buying and cooking of food is important not only to the physical needs of your family but also to its *emotional* well-being. For some women, cooking is an easy part of their lives. They do it naturally. But for me and many other women, cooking and the time involved can be a large obstacle in the smooth running of the household. Even though I feel that I can keep up with most of the demands in my life, cooking the evening meal can push me right over the edge. I really have to work at organizing my meal planning and shopping to have enough time to cook a decent meal for my family. Even though I am naturally an organized person, I still don't want to cook! (Note: Because of the difficulty I have in cooking every day, I wrote a cookbook to help all of us with this challenge! It's called *12 Steps to Becoming a More Organized Cook.*)

By the way, have you ever had this exchange with your husband?

> Him: What's for dinner?
> Me: I haven't decided. What do you want?
> Him: I don't know. Whatever you want.
> Me: Well, I need some ideas! How about chicken and
>   vegetables?
> Him: No, I had chicken at lunch.
> Me: Then what do you think would be good to eat?
> Him: I don't know. Whatever you want.

I think this dialogue happens all across America! But someone in the family has to take charge and make concrete decisions so that our families will eat healthy and spend time together.

Here are some tips to help you as you shop for food, cook, and organize your kitchen. In this step toward becoming a more organized woman, we get down to the basics of running a household and taking care of the family. Begin to look at the planning, shopping, and cooking in simple ways instead of as monsters that can consume you. Start by writing down the best foods you could prepare for your family and go from there. Remember, cooking is a tangible way of showing your family that you love them.

PLAN MEALS AHEAD

For each night of the week, predetermine a set menu item or theme. Here's how I do it:

Mondays. I have found it best to cook a full meat-based meal on Monday night and make enough for leftovers. I usually double the recipe or add extra meat. Then I just add fresh vegetables and a salad for a full meal without having to cook from scratch every night.

Tuesdays. When our girls were younger they attended Awana at our church on Tuesday nights and had to leave early. That night I prepared a quick pasta dish they liked. Now, since we are empty nesters, we have leftovers but I add other items to make a complete meal.

Wednesdays. We have Bible study on Wednesday so this is my break during the week—we eat out before the studies. When my girls were at home, this was the night for leftovers from Monday night.

Thursdays. We usually eat Italian meals on this night because my family loves spaghetti, lasagna, etc. (You could have different themes such as Mexican or Chinese, or even rotate several themes.)

Fridays. When the girls were younger, we indulged on Fridays and let the girls order pizza. This was our family night, and ordering pizza became a special tradition for our family. I would make a salad so that the meal was balanced. Now, Fridays are our date night, so we go out.

Saturdays. I don't plan a particular meal for this night unless we are having company. If the weather's nice, we might cook out. Keeping this night flexible helps me in my planning.

Sundays. Both my husband and I love to eat out after church. However, if we have leftovers from the weekend, we might eat at home, or if it's warm we may bring something home for a picnic in the backyard. Either way, our noon meal is usually a complete meal, so Sunday night we have a light meal. When the girls were growing up, this is when they would help with cooking. They loved grilled cheese sandwiches or breakfast foods.

As you can see, having a pre-set dinner theme helps me decide what I will cook each night. It also helps me plan my grocery shopping.

I know some women who cook the same recipe each week on the same day. It makes their grocery shopping and cooking so much easier!

For another woman, Jenny Rosenstrach, keeping a daily dinner diary was helpful. She wrote a book, *Dinner: A Love Story*, which offers inspiration and game plans for the home cook at every level. When she started the daily dinner diary her main thought was, "How do I make dinner happen?" She pulled out a blank notebook and wrote down a lineup of everything she wanted to cook that week. Then she drew up a shopping list based on that lineup and went to the supermarket. As she says, it wasn't an original idea, but her plan-in-advance system worked. After a while, she had a realization:

> I had a new theory about dinner. I found that if I was eating well, there was a good chance that I was living well, too. When I prioritized dinner, a lot of other things seemed to fall into place: We worked more efficiently to get out of our offices on time; we had a dedicated time and place to unload whatever was annoying us about work and everything else; and we spent less money by cooking our own food, which meant we never felt guilty about treating ourselves to dinner out on the weekend. And perhaps most important, the simple act of carving out the ritual gave every day purpose and meaning, no matter what else was going on in our lives.

I couldn't have said it better! Having a family meal each day is so important. In fact, a University of Michigan study found that meal time at home was the single strongest predictor of higher achievement scores and fewer behavioral problems among children. Meal time with the whole family gathered was found to be more valuable than time spent in activities such as school, studying, and playing sports.

However, realize that each week may be different for your family. Check each member's schedule for the upcoming week. Find out which days your husband may be out of town or have an evening meeting, and which nights your children have late practices or rehearsals. Plan to eat out on the really crazy nights when everyone is busy. Here are some tips that I hope will help you.

SHOP EFFICIENTLY

Shopping can become addictive and a tremendous time waster. Designate one day a week for shopping. You can also use this day for other shopping errands. I like to grocery shop, go to the post office, bank, dry cleaners, and a general store like Target in one day. If that is too much shopping for one day for you, have a day designated for groceries and another for clothes, presents, errands, etc. Make good lists of everything you need to do, keeping in mind where the stores are located in your town. If you plan your shopping trips, you will save gas and time. By keeping your shopping to a particular day, your week will be freed up for things you want to do. Jumping in the car for little things ends up taking big chunks of time out of your life as well as costing you more on gas.

Use coupons. If your grocery store markets double-coupons, you could easily save eight to fifteen dollars a week. This is a great way to be a good steward as well as helping with finances.

- Cut coupons and make your grocery list at the same time. I like to grocery shop on Mondays. On Sunday night, I sit down with the coupon sections from the paper and cut out new coupons. I then go through my other coupons and set aside the ones I will use at the store the next day. Then I make my grocery list, incorporating the coupons with it.

- Years ago, I separated and stored my coupons by category. Never again! Trying to keep up with all the coupons took too much time. Now I keep my coupons in one envelope with a rubber band around them. I can look through the whole stack in a few minutes, pull out the ones I want to use and I'm ready to go. (If you're Internet-savvy, check Valupage .com; RetailMeNot.com; Coupon-Lady.com; SmartMoney .com; TheKrazyCouponLady.com or CouponMom.com for coupons.)

When preparing your grocery list, check your master calendar and decide which nights you need to cook. List the meal you want to prepare for each night and pull those recipes. (This would be a good time to add those recipes that are special to your family on the days that work the best.) Then make your grocery list from these recipes.

Sort through your recipes and pull out your favorite ten or fifteen to use on a regular basis. Pull out recipes that are *yours,* that is, those you enjoy making and ones people identify with you. This tip has really helped me. I had been trying to cook everything I saw in the food section of the newspaper and my cookbooks! Don't get bogged down with a lot of cookbooks unless it's your hobby. Stack these favorite recipes near your shopping list and it will make your weekly planning much easier.

Arrange your grocery list to follow the layout of your grocery store. You will finish your grocery shopping faster without backtracking.

Buy according to the sales. Read the store ads in your newspaper and plan your menus accordingly. For example, if boneless chicken breasts are on sale, use recipes that need chicken breasts. You can save up to 40 percent simply by buying sale items.

Keep a grocery list on the refrigerator door or a convenient place. Show it to family members and tell them to write down items that are needed. This is especially helpful when your children become teenagers. Many times my daughter cooked or made a snack, using items without my knowledge. If she wrote these on the grocery list, I knew to buy them. Encourage family members to list anything else they need as well, such as school supplies or presents for a birthday party. Keeping this list has been a real time saver for me.

As soon as you open a new container, such as peanut butter or margarine, add it to your grocery list. That way, it will be bought and stored in the pantry or refrigerator until it's needed. Nothing is as frustrating as needing mayonnaise for a turkey sandwich, only to realize that the jar is empty and there's none in the pantry! Instead, buy things early and store them away. If you plan to buy before you need an item, you can wait until it's on sale or you have a coupon. More importantly, though, remember that needing items you don't have forces you to make time-wasting extra trips to the store. The list forewarns you so you can stay organized.

Keep emergency products on hand. Always make sure you have such items as water, powdered milk for snow days, bread in the freezer, and flashlights and batteries in the kitchen and each bedroom.

If you have very young children, grocery shop at night after they are in bed and your husband is there to watch them. This way you can shop without crying children. It will also free up your day so you can spend more quality time with them at home or at the park—unless, of course, the shopping trip is your outing together for that day. Usually, though, I preferred shopping without the children because I could shop faster and was able to concentrate better.

Shop for special holiday dinners or for company the day before you have to cook. That way you avoid shopping, cooking, and cleaning all in one day and won't be as tired.

PLAN YOUR COOKING AND
CONCENTRATE ON NUTRITION

We have to plan anything we want to do well, and cooking is no different. If we don't plan, we won't have groceries bought or meals cooked. And one of the most important aspects of cooking is building relationships with your family and friends in addition to fueling their bodies. Food brings people together, forms memories, and is a way to share our love.

We must also concentrate on *what* we are cooking. America's waistline is growing. An August 13, 2012, report from the Centers for Disease Control and Prevention found that more than a *third* of U.S. adults were obese and the number of states with a very high percentage of obese adults has reached 12. (*For more infor-mation, see Step 7.*)

Many experts believe there is a correlation between the rise in obesity among Americans and the staggering increase in diabetes, which has reached epidemic proportions. The same study showed that people with type 2 diabetes have the common characteristic of obesity.

What this means is that the health of our country is on the decline. Our children are beginning to have a shorter lifespan than their parents!

Please let this be a wakeup call. We must cut soft drinks, packaged foods, and fast food from our diets and replace them with fresh vegetables, fruits, nuts, beans, fish, and lean meats. I know it's easy to put a package of potato chips in your child's lunch, but it will harm him in the long run. Take the time to prepare fresh food instead and the health of your family will greatly improve.

Cook simply. Instead of using ten ingredients making a side salad that takes an hour, cut up fresh fruit or have a simple tossed salad. Instead of making a complex casserole, broil fish or meat in the oven and add fresh sautéed vegetables. If you don't want to spend a lot of time cooking, you really don't have to.

Cook healthy and good-tasting food. Always try to cook food that is in its natural state to avoid processed foods.

Every morning, know what you will be cooking for dinner that night. Nothing is worse than five o'clock approaching without having a clue what you will cook. If the meal is planned, you can pick up missing ingredients when you are out during the day. I try to incorporate this one tip every time I speak, and I have had many women say that it has saved their lives and their marriages! Planning really will help your life.

Try designating one day a week to cook. As I said, I like to cook on Mondays and use some of what I cooked or froze later in the week. Consider cooking one large piece of meat such as a ham, roast, or turkey breast and then serving it with different vegetables for different meals during the week. That way you are not starting from scratch each night.

Designate one day a month as a baking day. Bake breads, muffins, and cookies to freeze. I have a poppy seed bread recipe, which people seem to love that freezes well, so I set aside some time to bake it. I can usually make twenty-one loaves at one time. I wrap each one with aluminum foil, place it in a freezer bag, and label it. Then I'm ready for Christmas gifts, house guests, someone who is sick, or a special treat for my family.

Consider cooking with a friend. Buy your food in quantities and cook two or three freeze-proof recipes together. Double or triple recipes and freeze. Then these meals will be ready whenever you have a busy day, or if you need to give a meal to someone else. We are not always free to cook for that sick friend or new neighbor, so having a dish already in the freezer helps. I have a casserole recipe that I bake in batches, then label and freeze. It is also nice to have a meal in the freezer when you return from a trip.

Use ziplock freezer bags to freeze foods. That way, the baking dishes you prefer to use won't be in the freezer for a long time. Disposable aluminum pans work well also. Use square or rectangular shapes instead of round ones. They are easier to stack in your freezer and save space.

Use a slow cooker. This can free up your time when you are gone all day and want dinner ready when you come home. Put recipe ingredients in the slow cooker in the morning and you will have a wonderful dinner that night.

Use cooking bags. I have really enjoyed using these the last few years. I even use them to cook my Thanksgiving turkey. You can put meat and vegetables in the bag and the cooking time is much shorter than regular cooking. The best part? When you are ready to clean up, just throw the bag away—the pan will still be clean. Use a cooking bag when taking a dish to a sick friend. There are no dishes to return, and turkey breast or roasted chicken is a nice alternative to the basic lasagna casserole.

Become friends with your butcher. His advice on how to cook different kinds of meat and fish can be helpful. You can also ask him to cut steak into strips or cubes for Stroganoff or shish kebobs.

Enlist family help. They can help in the decision-making process of "What's for dinner?" and they can help cook. As your children get older, have them help you with the meals. Even small children can help with simple tasks. The best time to have them begin cooking is a weekend meal when you are not in such a hurry. My children started to cook on Sunday nights. My husband supervised and I got a break. Don't hesitate to delegate. You just can't do it all.

Don't feel guilty if you need breaks on certain days. I like to go out to eat after I've cooked a few days in a row. It gives me a lift and frees my afternoons up for other projects.

Along with cookbooks, use websites and apps to help you. One popular website is EatRight.org. It has info on nutrition and food safety as well as special sections for vegetarians, athletes, and other groups. Other popular sites to try are AllRecipes.com and Epicurious.com. MealBoard is an app that lets you plan your meal for the week and automatically generates your grocery list, and Grocery Pal organizes your grocery shopping and points you toward weekly specials from stores in our area.

ORGANIZE YOUR KITCHEN

One solution that can help with your daily cooking is getting your kitchen organized. I have such a hard time if I can't find anything. Go through your kitchen with the eyes of a time manager. Rearrange items for better efficiency. Where do you make sack lunches? Put bread knives and baggies close by, along with a cutting board. Where do you do most of your cutting? Have your sharp knives nearby. Dishes and glasses need to be close to the dishwasher, and pots and pans near the stove. Some of these suggestions are obvious, but sometimes we do things inefficiently out of habit. Take a new look at your kitchen and organize it to be a better work area.

Open all cabinets, step back and view where everything is. This step helps me visualize where I could rearrange items.

Then go through your cabinets and clear out everything you don't use, especially expired foods, old spices, and even plastic containers without lids. Streamline every drawer and cabinet. Use silverware holders, shelves, hooks, etc.

Clean out everything under your sink, leaving just what you use regularly. A plastic tub with low sides placed under the sink is a great way to keep your cleaning supplies together and in order. Keep a fresh sponge and counter cleaner handy and wipe counters down after every meal. This one simple task will make your kitchen look and smell clean all the time.

If you need extra storage in your kitchen, look for stacking units that come on casters. You can roll them wherever they are needed. Browse through kitchen stores and stores like The Container Store. They're full of organizing helps. Since the kitchen is the hardest area to run efficiently, this might be the best place to start your home organizing effort.

Delegate kitchen chores to your family. They can all help clean the kitchen and put their dishes in the dishwasher.

When your oven starts to look bad, clean it as soon as you can. The longer you wait, the harder the job gets.

Unload your dishwasher at night before you go to bed. As you unload, set out breakfast dishes. This way you'll be ahead in the morning and you can load the dishwasher before you head out for your day. If I didn't do this, my breakfast dishes might stay in the sink all day long.

Keep liquid soap by your sink at all times so you will be able to wash your hands and your children's easily and consistently. Use paper towels instead of cloth towels when their hands are very dirty, such as after school.

Bringing home Step 8

Whatever your hand finds to do, do it with all your might.

ECCLESIASTES 9:10

As the verse above says, we need to work as hard as we can on every task we encounter along the path to becoming more organized. And cooking for family and loved ones is vital to their welfare and our home life.

For Further Reflection

1. What method do you use to plan meals and shop for food?

2. Share some of your money-saving tips for shopping.

3. Do you have any tried and true—and easy—recipes?

4. How do you organize your kitchen?

5. How important is it for your family to eat together? What are some ways you can make this happen?

Personal Application

Finding the time and energy to cook for your family may be the most difficult part of your life. I know it is for me. So perhaps now might be a good time for reflection. What are some ways that you can help your family eat more healthily and economically? Perhaps you could find some new recipes that incorporate these benefits and try them out for your family this week. Perhaps along with new recipes, you could think of some ways to make meal time more of an exciting and anticipated event. Family members could take turns highlighting their day or choosing a topic for discussion. You could even plan to play a game or take a walk after the family meal.

Please know that even if you can't cook every night, it's important to plan *time* together for your family meal. You can have a family meal whether you cook or not, just by planning what take-home dishes everyone would like or going to a restaurant.

A WOMAN WHO WANTS TO BECOME MORE ORGANIZED ...

Manages the Details of Her Home

Teach the young women ... to be discreet, chaste, keepers at home, good, ... that the Word of God be not blasphemed.

TITUS 2:3-5 KJV

Changing her house into a home can be one of the most fulfilling goals a woman can have. Even if you are not the type of person who likes to clean, or you don't consider yourself a homemaker, you probably love the warm feeling you get when you welcome your family and friends to your home. Just think about Christmas. Imagine a tree all aglow with bright lights and presents overflowing near a roaring fire in the fireplace. The fire casts a golden haze of light on the windows revealing snowflakes floating down. The smell of freshly baked breads and cookies drifts in from the kitchen.

Yes, when my home is full of good food, beautiful decorations, and loved ones, I have a true sense of contentment and fulfillment. My goal is to have this same holiday contentment in my home every day. It takes work, time, effort, and even wisdom. Our homes are built by understanding how to keep a house in functioning order and how to keep the people inside together and united.

In Titus 2:5 Paul tells us to be "sensible, pure, workers at home." This verse reveals one of the goals the Lord has for us as wives and homemakers: being hard workers in our homes. On the other hand, we also need to remember what the psalmist says, "Unless the LORD builds the house, they labor in vain who build it" (Psalm 127:1 NKJV). In other words, we need to put the Lord first in our lives and in our home-building. If we follow His guidelines, we will succeed with this goal.

I know that there are many women who may struggle with feelings of inadequacy or label themselves as "just a homemaker." Our society seems to glorify those who are in the shine of the spotlight: the unwed movie star moms, the bachelorettes, and reality stars. We see pictures on magazine covers of these beautiful, rich, and successful women who don't seem to have a care in the world. It appears that they aren't buying groceries, cooking dinner, and staying up late with a sick child! But whenever you feel that way, realize that there are also many women who know that building a home and growing the next generation is the most valuable occupation they could ever choose. Stephen R. Covey, author of *The 7 Habits of Highly Effective People,* writes: "I think the most significant work we'll do in our whole life, in our whole world, is done within the four walls of our home."

The Proverbs 31 woman "[looked] well to the ways of her household." She would have to be organized to do so. And as verse 27 says, she wasn't idle or lazy. She acted with purpose and did her very best to take care of her household.

Just as the Proverbs and Titus 2 women did, you too can "look well to the ways of your household." I know keeping a house is difficult, especially when there are children to take care of. Though there are many helpful tips here, remember that the best tip is you! Just get up and do the very best you can every day. Ask yourself, "What kind of home will I build today?"

ORGANIZE YOUR HOME

The hardest part of organizing is getting started. If you're struggling to get started, remember that organizing reduces stress. Reduced stress means more joy and peace in your life. Even though starting this new project of organizing your home is hard, the benefits far outweigh the hardships!

First, walk through your house and determine what room should be organized first, second, and so on. This allows you to focus on the whole house and gives you the chance to visualize what you want. Then make a list of these rooms and promise yourself you will give each room one week. It may not take this long, but by giving yourself a week you make a commitment to get it done thoroughly. Breaking down the task room by room will make organizing your house more manageable.

As you go from room to room, consider which of these three things you will want to do with each room:

- Organize
- Decorate
- Clean

Don't forget to also list smaller areas, such as closets, the kitchen pantry, or the laundry room, that need reorganizing. Try scheduling one a week until they are all finished.

If you notice that space is a problem as you walk through your home, begin to think of ways you can make your rooms multi-task. For example, one room could serve as your office, TV room, and guest room (a pullout sofa works perfectly for the few times you may have overnight guests). Your family room can also serve as a play room for your children. Simply move your sofa further into the room and set up a play area behind it. If you don't have room for that, dedicate a corner of the family room for their toys.

Your bedroom could have a comfortable chair or chaise lounge in a corner for your reading area.

As you go through your house room by room, consider which of these four things you will do with every item in that room:

- Keep it if you use it (and then give each item you keep a home—a place where it will always be).
- Give it away if you don't.
- Sell it in a garage sale, on Craigslist.com, or to a friend.
- Throw it away!

We have too much stuff cluttering our homes. The more we have, the more we are responsible for.

There are three ways to organize the items in every space:

- Shelves
- Hooks
- Bins and small trays/plastic boxes and canisters

These few items can revolutionize your home. Let me give you some examples.

Shelves can be used in every room and closet in your home as well as your garage and attic. These can be built-in or bought inexpensively at places like Lowe's, Home Depot, Target, or Walmart. The purpose of shelves is to put like items together off the floor, which will reduce clutter. As you walk through your home, visualize where shelving could be used for your children's toys and sport equipment; your sewing or hobby items; holiday decorations; laundry and cleaning items; tools; garden and yard items; books and DVDs; pictures; home office items; or extra kitchen needs. There are even shelves that can slide out, which are a huge help in the kitchen or in your office for your printer.

Hooks are another way to organize. Use them on the back of doors, such as in your bathrooms for towels, nightgowns, and robes. I use hooks for the towels I use daily so that the towels on the bathroom rods always look nice. Use hooks in the laundry room for beach towels, sweaters and jackets, and shopping bags. Every closet in your home could use hooks for clothes you use daily, such as nightwear, as well as for purses, belts, and travel kits. Hooks are great for garages and attics too.

Bins are items I couldn't live without! I store so many things in them: holiday decorations; children's art projects and special awards; out-of-season clothes; family pictures or keepsakes; kitchen items; electrical cords/ computer items; art supplies; desk supplies; mail, forms, letters, bills; beach or pool items; batteries; light bulbs; and dog food and dog toys. What works best is to place items in a plastic bin and then place it on a shelf. Remember too that these bins come in all sizes and shapes. When I was growing up, all we had to organize our stuff in was cardboard boxes! Now, there are hundreds of shapes and sizes for any need you may have.

Think creatively about where you can use bins around the house. The clear ones are perfect for office supplies. Clear trays work great in the refrigerator for keeping condiments together and saving shelf space. I use a plastic bin under my kitchen and bathroom sinks to hold cleaning supplies, rubber gloves, and sponges. It's great to just reach into a cabinet and retrieve an item I want without having to search for it! I also use a bin with a cover for restaurant coupons. We keep this one in the car for whenever we decide to eat out. Don't forget your kitchen and bathroom closets, either. You can store all your pasta, beans, flour, cereals, crackers, and other pantry items in clear plastic storage units or canisters that will keep order as well protect the food from air. For the bathroom, organized storage can keep your Kleenex, cotton balls, Q-tips, soaps, makeup, and so forth neat and easy to get to.

I also suggest using dividers for drawers in the kitchen, office, and bathroom—they can really help keep your items organized. Some of these have plastic interlocking inserts so you can adjust their sizing.

I know that some of you may be feeling overwhelmed by all these ideas, but don't be discouraged. Remember I suggested taking about a week per area to get organized? Take your time planning what you want to do. Then, take your time in purchasing the organizing items you want to use. Look for when they go on sale. If doing a whole room is too much, then organize one shelf, one file, or one drawer at a time. Every little bit adds up to a completed area. Remember: Rome wasn't built in a day and neither are our homes!

Make a commitment to be disciplined with the organization of your home. Sometimes the easy part is working on a room and getting it finished. But the hard part is keeping up with the organization daily so that your home doesn't get cluttered again. The best advice I can give you is to make a commitment to yourself to pick up and put things away as soon as you use them. Once this becomes a habit, you will find that keeping up your home becomes much easier. You may also want to see what Scripture says about working hard. Ants are held up by wise King Solomon as an example of industry: "Go to the ant, you sluggard! Consider her ways and be wise, which, having no captain . . . provides her supplies in the summer, and gathers her food in the harvest" (Proverbs 6:6-8 NKJV). God uses His creatures to instruct us. From the ant, we can see the importance of planning ahead and laying away provisions for the future (Proverbs 30:25).

Determine to stay on top of the rooms that continue to get disorganized. Concentrate most of your time on these rooms. For me, the kitchen and my office are the hardest areas to keep orderly and clean. I have had to adjust my expectations and clear them of clutter as consistently as I can.

When organizing your kitchen, you might want to clean out the cabinets and drawers, clean the shelves, and add fresh shelf paper. Perhaps you need to rearrange some cabinets. Periodically, I clean out my cabinets and pantry, removing unused, outdated foods and reorganizing items. (*For more tips on kitchen organization, see Step 8.*)

When you move into a new home, use these same tips. With paper and pen, walk through each room of the house and decide which room should be unpacked first. Leave the boxes in the other rooms and don't worry about them.

- If you have to sleep in the new house the first night, pack and label one box with all the first night essentials (beds and bedding, coffee and the coffee pot, towels, soap and tissue for the bathroom) so the necessities can be unpacked first.

- Unpack the kitchen first, bathrooms next, then bedrooms.

- List which rooms need shelves, drapes, blinds, and so on. By placing these needs on a list, you can decide what should be done first, and you won't be overwhelmed.

Organizing isn't just putting in order. It's also developing your house to fit your particular style. And there aren't any right or wrong styles. When you begin to put together your home, you can use all your creative ideas to make your home a haven for you and your family. If you have a budget for it, ask a home decorator to visit your home and help with ideas. Many furniture stores offer this service for free.

CLEAN EFFECTIVELY

There are hundreds of books on cleaning. The best tip I can give you is that cleaning a house can be simple and does not need to take all day. But it does take organization! Staying organized will keep your home cleaner and in order day by day.

Walk through your home again, and this time, try to look at it with fresh eyes—the way guests will see it. You may notice dust you never knew was there, fingerprints on the doorjambs, a broken knob on a kitchen cabinet, wall paper peeling, or stains on the carpet. Write these down and then decide when you can tackle them.

Decide on a weekly cleaning plan. I have a two-story house. Once a week, I clean the downstairs at night (vacuum, mop the kitchen floor, dust, and clean the half-bath). The next morning, I do the upstairs and am usually finished by noon. My family helps, so I can't take all the credit. When my husband is in town, he vacuums. The girls help dust and clean their bathrooms. There is no guilt in hiring housekeeping help. For women who work outside the home or mothers with preschoolers, this may be the best option for your sanity!

Devise a quick way to do necessary daily cleaning. I straighten the downstairs before I go to bed at night (unload the dishwasher, take out the newspaper, adjust pillows on the sofa). The next morning I straighten the upstairs (wipe down bathroom counters, make beds, take trash and dirty clothes downstairs). I call this morning routine my "five-minute quick clean." I recommend one every morning and night. If a house is "quick cleaned" daily, the once-a-week heavy cleaning won't take nearly as long. Your own quick clean may sometimes take longer than five minutes, but it will still be a big help to you.

To "quick clean" simply means to quickly put your house in order daily. Wipe kitchen and bathroom counters, take down dirty towels and add fresh ones, empty trash cans, empty dirty clothes hampers, and make beds. Check children's rooms for dirty clothes, and for curling irons, lights, and radios left on. Begin a load of laundry, sweep the kitchen floor, and load the dishwasher. In less than forty-five minutes, your house is set for the day. (To save time, I work while talking on the phone. In fact, I usually do something around the house while on the phone.)

Clear up the clutter. Remember that clutter is what makes a house look messy. In fact, 40 percent of cleaning a house is getting rid of clutter. Clutter causes stress. Remove as much clutter as you can before you begin to clean. You will be able to clean much faster. And don't be afraid to throw out or give this stuff away. Focus first on high-use areas—spaces you need to clear in order to get through your day efficiently—such as the desk where you pay bills. Next, tackle the places you ignore. If there's a drawer that makes you wince every time you open it, remind yourself that it's probably less taxing to sort through it than to feel frustrated every day.

Understand that clutter can be emotional. I want each one of you to know that I understand how difficult controlling your clutter may be. You don't have to be a pathological hoarder to have a problem with material belongings. We all may have that impulse to nest and collect. But sometimes it can go wrong, especially in our culture where there's constant pressure to acquire things and to define ourselves by our possessions. We also may tend to hoard if we have lost a loved one, moved to another house, or had another major change in one's life. If organizing all your stuff is too difficult for you, ask a friend to help. And realize that you aren't alone. Storage units are built daily across this country to give all our "stuff" room. Just know that although your many items have emotional meaning, you are devoting a huge amount of energy to what is really just "stuff."

Wisdom from others. If you need some extra encouragement with organizing your home, read some of the experts. Gretchen Rubin writes a monthly column for *Good Housekeeping*. She also wrote *Happier at Home.* She writes, "As I cleared clutter, I felt a growing sense of peace. Nothing is more satisfying than a home that works easily and well."

Sweep once a day, either after breakfast or after you have done the dinner dishes. This will keep the rest of the house cleaner because crumbs and dirt won't get tracked through the house.

Every day, clean your counters in the kitchen and bathroom with a specific product for that purpose. It only takes a few seconds, but they will look wonderful and will be germ-free. Use rubber gloves when you clean. You won't mind cleaning nearly as much.

Have cleaning supplies in every bathroom, or put your cleaning supplies in a bucket and carry it with you to all the bathrooms.

Keep a roll of paper towels and a spray cleaner under each sink so everyone can help with cleaning. To keep the showers clean, keep a spray bottle of cleaner (I use Clean Shower) in the shower. Whoever uses the shower sprays the walls, doors, and floor upon exiting.

Schedule your major cleaning for the same day each week. Your house will stay neat regularly. This is how women cleaned many years ago. Each day of the week was designated for one particular task: Monday was usually wash day, Tuesday was baking day, and so forth.

Use the old-fashioned "spring cleaning" for big jobs in your house such as windows, carpets, and washing blankets. If you know you will have a specific time each year to do these harder jobs, you won't worry about them the rest of the year.

Hire outside help. If you who work full time, I suggest getting others to come in and help you with the house cleaning. You really can't do it all! One time when I suggested this at a speaking engagement, a woman with six children asked if it was all right for her to get help. I answered with a very enthusiastic yes! She had felt guilty about hiring a cleaner since she was a stay-at-home mom. I feel that she is a full-time worker! She later wrote me and said this one tip had saved her life.

If your children won't pick up their shoes or toys, throw the items into a plastic bin or box and charge them twenty-five cents to get the items back. This teaches children their clutter is their responsibility, not yours.

Put a doormat by the exterior doors and make everyone wipe their feet each time they come into the house. I have discovered that this is the best way to keep shoes clean and the rest of your house free from dirt and dust. You will also be protecting your carpets and helping them last longer. Of course, taking off shoes works best, but some people don't care to do that.

Eat meals and snacks in your kitchen or dining room. This will keep your sofas, chairs, and carpets much cleaner and save you hours of cleaning time and money. For the television room, keep popcorn on hand. Air-popped popcorn isn't messy and is great when watching movies.

Measure how much time a particular job takes to do. For example, I don't like to fold clothes. So I timed it once and discovered one large load of white clothes took ten minutes to fold. That isn't very long. Now that I know that, I don't mind folding clothes as much!

Give yourself time limits for each job with a reward at the end. For example, if I can clean my upstairs by eleven, I stop and take my walk or read the newspaper. I find I always work better and faster if there is something I want to do when I am finished.

SAFETY MEASURES FOR YOUR HOME

As you organize your home, create a personal safety net in case of an emergency. We never know when a tornado, hurricane, or other emergency may strike. Here are some ideas.

Set a part of your home (your "safe room") for your emergency items. In case of a tornado warning, choose the basement, an inside closet or bathroom where you and your family agree beforehand to meet. In case of a flood, choose to meet on a higher level.

Create a first-aid kit and check expiration dates yearly. It could contain: sterile gloves, dressing, adhesive bandages, a multipurpose pocket knife, soap, antibiotic ointment, burn ointment, eyewash, a thermometer, aspirin/pain reliever, antacid, anti-diarrhea medication, laxative, sanitation items such as toilet paper, plastic bags, hand wipes or hand sanitizer, toothbrushes, toothpaste, spare glasses or contact lenses, and hearing aid batteries.

Essential papers. Copy important documents and stash them with money in a sealed container. Consider backing up the following records electronically: emergency contact information of family, friends, doctors, and insurers; ID cards such as photo IDs, passports, health insurance, Social Security; family records such as birth, marriage, death certificates; medical and immunization records, prescriptions; wills, insurance policies, contracts, deeds, or leases; recent tax returns; bank and credit card statements, retirement account records, investment records; local maps; video or photos of your valuables and the interior and exterior of your home.

Create a ready-to-go container with important items (along with your first-aid kit and essential papers): one gallon of water per person, per day, 3-day supply; food, nonperishable, ready-to-eat items; pet food, 3-day supply; manual can opener; whistle; battery-powered or hand-crank radio; flashlight and batteries; spare cell phone chargers; cell phone charger for your car (in case of loss of electricity); extra set of car and house keys; matches in waterproof container; blankets; extra clothing, hat, sturdy shoes, toys for your children. (Note on how to treat non-bottled water for drinking: After filtering water through clean cloths, add 8 drops of regular household liquid bleach to 1 gallon of water. If water is cloudy or muddy, add 16 drops.)

Stay-home container. In case you are stranded in your own home, use the same items as the to-go container but also add: 14-day supply of water and food; fire extinguisher; work gloves; face masks for dust and mold; tool box; plastic sheeting and duct tape for sealing windows, doors; chlorine bleach with medicine dropper; extra blankets, sleeping bags; and rain ponchos and towels.

If you own a smartphone, load apps or bookmarks for your bank, insurance company, the Red Cross, FEMA, the website of the National Weather Service, and local news outlets.

If you back up your computer to an external hard drive, store the drive in your safe room and not in the room with your computer.

In case of fire, tell all family members where to meet and have escape plans established. You may even want to purchase a fire-escape ladder.

You may also want to keep your home safe from burglars: Keep bushes cut low; plant thorny shrubs below ground-floor windows; install flood lights; use heavy-duty deadlock bolts; get a security system; store valuables in your child's sock drawer rather than in the master bedroom; and keep your car keys next to your bed while you sleep. If you hear a suspicious noise and suspect that someone is trying to break in, press the Panic button on your key ring. The car alarm will sound!

If you are going away on vacation, ask a neighbor to get your mail, newspaper, and any flyers left on your front door. Don't load the car up the night before unless it can be placed in a garage. If you have workers inside your home, check and make sure the windows haven't been unlocked.

As you begin to organize your home, remember what the goal is. The goal is taking small steps in different areas that result in the large step of becoming more organized. A well-managed home does take work, but the end result is less stress and more time for you and the family you love. With God's help, you can do it.

CREATE A PEACEFUL HOME

Do you want a godly home? A home that is governed by God and run with efficiency and order? Then think about these suggestions from *A Godly Home* by Joyce Meyer:

Speak in vocal tones that bring peace. Avoid screaming and yelling; avoid being harsh.

Build each other up. Don't tear each other down. Don't criticize. Be positive, not negative.

Work together to keep order. Teach your children to pick up after themselves.

Laugh! Laughter is medicine to your soul. Have fun together often and regularly.

Be slow to anger, slow to speak, quick to hear. Be a good listener. Forgive each other. Have mercy for other's faults. God has certainly forgiven us, so we should forgive others.

Don't be overly sensitive. Often family members say things that hurt us without intending any harm.

Do not judge. Each person in a family goes through different problems because of their age, circumstances, health, and stress.

Don't say "Hurry up!" all the time. This one phrase can steal such peace and joy. Organize your schedule so you have more time.

Don't worry. If your mind isn't peaceful, your unrest will infiltrate your life and home.

Make your house a member of the family. In other words, your house should be a home, a refuge from the world. It should be a place of warmth where family pictures are hung, where everyone contributes to its care, and where friends can visit. (This thought is from *Seven Highly Effective Secrets for a Family* by Stephen R. Covey.)

You can guard your home by keeping it full of the Word of God. Whether you're organizing your closets or working on family relationships, ask God to help you make your work reflect His glory. And just as you are working and building up your home, so is the Lord building you up.

> You also, like living stones, are being built into a spiritual house to be a holy priesthood, offering spiritual sacrifices acceptable to God through Jesus Christ. (1 Peter 2:5 NIV)

To end this section, I wanted to share with you a beautiful anonymous poem I quote each time I speak:

The Home Beautiful

The Crown of the Home is Godliness
The Beauty of the Home is Order
The Glory of the Home is Hospitality
The Blessing of the Home is Contentment.

ORGANIZING CLOTHES AND CLOSETS

Clothes. We can't live without them. But they do take a lot of time and effort. Eve had it easy until she ate that apple!

Now don't get me wrong. I love clothes. I love to wear something new, to have accessories that really complement an outfit, to have new shoes, and to look the best I can. However, there is one problem: I don't like to shop and I don't have the time. Taking care of my family's clothing needs is hard for me. I usually catalogue shop for myself, which can be fast and simple. But keeping up with the clothes my family needs takes more time and effort. And I think a lot of women share my feelings.

There is no sin in being the best we can be for God and our family. We should glorify God in every area of life. This requires a balanced approach toward things that, if taken to extremes, can distract us from Him. First Peter 3:3 reminds us, "your adornment must not be merely external—braiding the hair, and wearing gold jewelry . . ." Peter wasn't forbidding women from styling their hair or wearing jewelry at all; he just didn't want women to be as preoccupied with those things as they were in Roman society. Peter was saying that we need a healthy balance in our lives.

When I was a little girl, my mother made just about everything my sisters and I wore. I remember coming home after school and seeing my mother and my grandmother going through all the clothes that had been stored away. They let out hems or took up hems from hand-me-downs. It was a great way to save money but it also showed me the value of reusing clothing. My mother and grandmother taught me, by their hard work ethic, how to take care of clothes. They were an example for me when I began to take care of my children's clothes. We never left the house without looking clean and well taken care of, from our shoes to how our hair looked. Mother helped us develop a good self-image because of the time and effort she put into helping us look our best.

This is an important point. It does take a tremendous amount of time and effort to have your children look their best. As you become more organized in your home and life, you'll find the extra time to keep up with their clothes and hair. You will also have time to show your children how to take care of their clothes and themselves as they get older. And as you practice some of the tips I list below, you will save money and time.

DEVELOP A METHOD FOR SORTING
AND STORING CLOTHES

Did you know that 80 percent of American women (2012 report from Consumers Report) leave at least a quarter of the items in their closets unused? That sounds like a waste of perfectly good space and clothes to me! Here are some tips to reduce that statistic.

Twice a year, exchange a season of clothes in your closets and drawers. In late summer or early fall, pull out all the summer items, sort them, place them in storage and replace them with your winter clothes. In early spring, remove the heavy winter items from your closet and replace them with spring and summer ones. Beyond just than keeping your closets clean and organized, this process also helps you know what you need to buy. You will save money you would have spent buying items you don't really need for yourself or your children. When I remove a season from a closet, I put the clothes in five piles:

- Laundry

- Dry cleaning

- Mending

- Give away

- Ready to be stored

Make a habit of regularly going through your young children's closets and drawers to straighten and organize too. You will be able to see if more clothes are needed, and what needs cleaning or mending. When my children were younger, I sometimes found dirty, worn clothes back on their shelves. I discovered I needed to check their closets regularly. By keeping up on their closets and drawers, the twice-a-year switch from one season to another was not as difficult. As your children get older, teach them to become responsible in this same way.

Get rid of clothes that you haven't worn in three years. There are many people who are in real need of clothes. We should be willing to give clothes we don't use to others who would use them. This will also help to keep our closets streamlined and organized.

Go through all your stockings, belts, accessories, and jewelry to throw out old items and to reorganize the rest. Store the items you retain where you can find them at a moment's notice, fresh and ready. I place my pantyhose, still packaged, vertically in a small box in my closet. Each package is labeled with the color of pantyhose, so I can quickly find the pair I want. After wearing, I file the pantyhose back in the same package and back in the box. This suggestion may seem small, but even this little bit of organization simplifies my life.

Organize socks and underwear. These smaller items need a place too. You could stack them neatly in drawers or purchase bins to help you keep them neat. I have a drawer just for my bras, another for panties, and another for slips, etc. The time I save knowing where to find each item is invaluable.

Organize your belts on a hanger or buy a belt rack for your closet.

Organize hair bows. If you or your daughters use hair bows, you can clip them to a cloth belt and hang the belt on a hook or coat hanger. Then your bows are all in a beautiful, rainbow-colored line and you can find the color you want quickly.

Buy plastic or cardboard storage bins to help organize out-of-season clothes. These can be placed on shelves or under a bed. These containers are also wonderful for storing prized heirlooms such as baby clothes.

Avoid plastic dry-cleaning bags for long-term storage. They trap moisture and encourage mildew. Instead, use fabric clothing bags or acid-free cardboard boxes, or cover clothing with old sheets.

Add blocks of cedar, boxes of scented candles, soap, or old perfume bottles to the closet to keep clothes smelling fresh. You can also tuck sweet-smelling sachets between clothes in closets and drawers.

At the end of the day, before putting your clothes away in a tightly packed closet, hang them where they can air out.

Buy hooks for everything and every place you need to organize. They are wonderful for the backs of bathroom and closet doors, and in the laundry room for coats and backpacks. Keep things off the floor and on shelves and hooks. Your home will look less cluttered and more open.

Buy an inexpensive cardboard cabinet with drawers for your closet to keep lingerie, socks, or accessories organized.

Buy closet expanders to increase how much your closet holds. These can be bought at most discount or building supply stores. You might also consider hiring a company such as California Closets to come to your home and redesign your closets. You will be amazed at the extra space you will have. It's well worth the price.

Have a specific drawer, shelf, or hook for each item. If you always keep your swimsuits, nightgowns, sweaters, and belts in the same place, you will be able to find what you need when you want it. You won't lose things as easily and you'll have less clutter.

Invest in better quality hangers. These are well worth the bit of extra money you'll spend. They make your closet look better too.

- Use large plastic colored hangers for most items. Your clothes will not be pressed as close together in the closet as they would be on wire hangers, so they will look better and need less ironing.

- Hang delicate garments on padded hangers whenever possible.

- Invest in pants hangers. Your pants will hang higher on the rod, leaving more space on the shelf or on the floor below for other storage.

Fold sweaters and store them on shelves or in drawers.

Don't forget your hall closet! Sort through the winter coats and jackets each spring and clean them, store them, or give them away. If you store cameras, equipment or other items on the shelf in this closet, buy plastic bins to organize. Add extra hangers for guests' coats.

BUY CLOTHES WISELY

The best time to buy new clothes is after you have sorted and stored away the clothes in your closets. You'll see what you need to replace or what you need to buy for the new season. Write down what each person in the family needs and your buying trip will go more quickly.

Be on the lookout for sales. Buy winter coats in January. Buy jeans and play clothes at discount stores. Stores such as Target, T.J. Maxx, Kohl's, and Walmart are a great source for basic family clothing needs such as gloves, hats, shirts, camp clothes, and swimming suits. The prices are usually much lower than at department stores and the quality is fine for children who are growing.

Though sales are wonderful, don't buy something just because it is on sale. Make sure you need the item. It is better to have one great outfit than a closet full of sale items you don't wear or need.

As your children get older, let them help you with their clothing purchases. Make shopping a fun outing! Let your children know that taking care of them is a joy and that their opinion about what they wear is important to you.

Let your older children have a clothing allowance. Then they can be responsible for the cost and the choice of their own clothes. This is a great tool for teaching them money management. And if they want something very expensive, such as a special type of shoe or purse, let them work and earn the money themselves for it.

If you enjoy sewing, make some of your family's clothes. This can help greatly with the finances. I love needlework, so I smocked dresses for my two daughters when they were little. It saved money on expensive dresses and my daughters remember me making them something special. The dresses will be heirlooms for them to keep. In fact, I saved these dresses and now my granddaughter is wearing them!

DEVELOP AN EFFICIENT METHOD FOR KEEPING CLOTHES CLEAN

Taking care of the clothes you already have is important if you want to be a good steward of your money and possessions. Your favorite clothes will last longer if you take good care of them.

Wash clothes on a regular basis. You don't want clothes to sit in heaps growing mildew. Pre-treat stains as soon as you can.

Have your family members pre-treat stains. Nothing is worse than sorting laundry and finding a stain that has been there too long. Make a rule that each person pre-treat the stain and then leave it so you can find it. At some point, your children should be doing their own laundry. Only you can determine what age is best for your children, but I think teenagers are old enough for this task. It's a mother's job to teach her children how to live on their own by the time they leave home.

Keep socks paired up. My father taught me this trick: using a safety pin, connect the heels of a pair of socks. They will stay

---

together in the wash so you won't have to sort them! Use a different color or size of pin for each family member or use clips such as Sock Cops (www.sockcop.com) to keep mates united through wash and dry.

Follow directions for your washer and dryer exactly. Select the best water temperature for each load. Always sort wash loads by color and fabric type. Never overload your washer or dryer. It can damage your machines and your clothes will not get as clean. Also, make sure you clean the lint trap *each* time you dry, and wipe or vacuum up any lint lining the lint flow area.

Follow directions for your detergent. Some newer machines require HE (High Efficiency) detergent and, yes, it makes a difference. Make sure to use the measuring lines on detergent caps. Too much soap will harm the machine and will not be completely rinsed out of your clothes.

Use the "quick wash" setting. If your clothes aren't really soiled, the quick wash setting will wash them in about half the time and save energy. I like to use this for lingerie or if a load has stayed in the washer too long and needs to refreshed.

Don't double up on drying. If you mix towels or jeans with lightweight garments, the latter will get overly dried while the dryer keeps going for the heavier ones. Drying two separate loads protects your clothes. Although my white towels could be washed in my white loads, I keep them separate.

Remove your clothes from the dryer before it stops. This reduces wrinkles. Another good tip: Let your knit shirts stay in the dryer for only a few minutes. Take them out while still damp, and hang them up on a wide hanger to dry. Smooth out wrinkles, and when they're dry they won't need any ironing. You can also lay items like shorts or slacks flat, smooth them out and they will not need ironing.

Fold clothes as soon as you can. Sometimes we can get in the habit of tossing dried clothes into a clothes basket and folding when we have the time. But this will mean all the clothes will be wrinkled. Instead, plan what time of day works best for you to wash, dry, and fold. One method that worked for me is to put in a wash as soon as I did my morning five-minute-quick clean. My next window of time was around lunch when I knew I would have time to put them in the dryer and hang or fold as they were ready. When I was working, I would do my wash while preparing dinner and then hang or fold watching the news before bedtime.

Use small bins for undies, socks, or tights. Instead of folding these items, toss them into bins for each family member, which then can be placed on a closet shelf or in the dresser drawer.

Use your dryer's automatic cycle. The sensors detect a load's moisture and stop the tumbling when contents are dry. If you don't have that option, then dry on the lowest heat setting. For towels, use the medium setting. The high setting can damage your clothes. If you can't adjust the heat setting, set a timer for around thirty minutes, which is about the time it takes for a light load to dry.

Keep your laundry area neat by using bins, shelves, and hooks. Keep a trash can there for the lint you remove from the dryer. Have special bins for different type of clothes to be washed: one for whites, one for darks, one for towels, and one for delicate or hand-washed items.

Make it a game. What I mean by this is, treat your laundry room as a challenge! My goal is to keep the bins of dirty clothes empty. Those of you with multiple children will never catch up with the dirty laundry, but by keeping up with it daily you will save yourself stress.

Have a special place (rod, bin, or hook) for clothes that need ironing. Then, have one set time each week to iron. I like to iron while I watch TV newscasts. I have a portable ironing board I place on the kitchen counter. Before I realize it, all my ironing is finished.

Tip for ironing delicates. If you place a handkerchief over the item, you can set the iron's temperature to match the fabric's most fragile fiber (such as nylon or silk) and iron over lace or other decorations.

Having said all that, remember what Jesus said about clothing in Matthew 6:28–29:

> And why are you worried about clothing? Observe how the lilies of the field grow; they do not toil nor do they spin, yet I say to you that not even Solomon in all his glory clothed himself like one of these.

Though taking care of our family's clothing needs is important, there are others things that are more important. "Strength and dignity are her clothing" (Proverbs 31:25). Instead of focusing completely on our clothes, we should be concerned with the beauty of our character. We should hope that our inner qualities are obvious to anyone who is with us. The Proverbs woman had this inner strength and dignity that was seen by others. She knew who was in charge of her life: the Lord. She had an eternal view of life instead of a temporal one. She could smile at the future because she knew her life and the lives of her family were in the hands of God.

> *Your beauty should not come from outward adornment,*
> *such as braided hair and the wearing of gold jewelry*
> *and fine clothes. Instead, it should be that of your*
> *inner self, the unfading beauty of a gentle and quiet*
> *spirit, which is of great worth in God's sight.*
> **1 PETER 3:3–4** NIV

Bringing home Step 9

She looks well to the ways of her household.

PROVERBS 31:27

Women tell me that maintaining their homes is in the most diffi-cult part of being more organized. But with a few helpful tips and some motivation, anyone can develop a more organized home, permeated with a godly flavor.

For Further Reflection

1. What do you think makes the difference between a house and a home? What are some ways you could make your house into a home?

2. Now might be a good time to walk through your home (ei-ther visually or physically) and decide how you could orga-nize, decorate, or clean each room in order to make your house a home. Write down your ideas and then begin taking action.

3. How could you implement the "five-minute quick clean" in your mornings? What would be a good day, each week, to do your heavy cleaning?

4. Clutter is the enemy of an organized home. What clutter could you get rid of in your home?

5. Think how businesses organize and schedule things. What are some ways you could organize and schedule the house responsibilities better?

6. What is the hardest part about keeping up with your fam-ily's clothes?

7. What ideas do you have for sorting and storing your clothes?

8. Do you have any special tips on cleaning and caring for your family's clothes?

Personal Application

- What are your overall goals for your home? Take time to think this through, then write these goals down.

- On a sheet of paper, map out the different rooms in your home. Write out your goals for each room.

- Don't forget to include your husband and children in these discussions. The whole family should help you with the up-keep of the home. Let them help decide on how their rooms can be decorated or where shelves should go for their activities and collections.

A WOMAN WHO WANTS TO BECOME MORE ORGANIZED ...

Nurtures and Provides for Her Children

Children are a gift of the LORD, the fruit of the womb is a reward.

PSALM 127:3

This chapter is probably my favorite. Nothing is more important to our lives and to the future than our children. Holding that new bundle brings such raw emotions: how are we going to take care of this tiny human being, feed them, care and nurture them, and raise them up in the knowledge of the Lord?

If nothing in this world gives us more joy than our children, nothing takes as much time and energy! Someone told me that children steal your heart so that even when they are grown adults, you still have deep emotional ties to them. God looks at children as precious gifts: the psalmist tells us that "children are a gift of the LORD, the fruit of the womb is a reward" (Psalm 127:3). If God says children are this special, then we should treat them as such. Jesus Himself rebuked the disciples when they tried to make a group of children go away:

Then some children were brought to Him so that He might lay His hands on them and pray; and the disciples rebuked them. But Jesus said, "Let the children alone, and do not hinder them from coming to Me; for the kingdom of heaven belongs to such as these." (Matthew 19:13–14)

Proverbs 31:26 offers us an example of how a mother should treat her children: "She opens her mouth in wisdom, and the teaching of kindness is on her tongue." We need to open our mouths in wisdom, not with constant criticism and put-downs, and to talk to our children with kindness, not with yelling and harsh words. This is a personal soap box for me. I hurt anytime I see a child mistreated. I know that raising kids has always been a challenge. Today, that task can feel more daunting than ever, so I know how hard it can be some days to be patient and loving. We will all lose it at times because none of us is perfect! I can remember looking at my husband and saying, "When are they leaving for college?!" But I know the Lord wants us to be as loving and gentle to our children as we can.

Our speech says a lot about us. It is through our words that we are deemed wise or foolish. Proverbs 16:20-25 contains insightful advice showing us how to talk to others. It says that we are to speak careful, judicious, right, and gracious words that are persuasive and pleasant to hear—words that bring encouragement and life. The apostle Paul, too, called for gracious and wise speech in Ephesians 4:29: "Do not let any unwholesome talk come out of your mouths, but only what is helpful for building others up according to their needs, that it may benefit those who listen" (NIV).

Mothers are the real teachers for their children. Proverbs 31:1 shows us that King Lemuel learned prophecy from his mother. In 2 Timothy 3:15, Paul said to Timothy, "From childhood you have known the sacred writings." Timothy had been taught by his mother and grandmother, as most Hebrew children were in biblical days. Daughters remained under their mother's guidance and teaching until their marriage. Sons were taught more and more by their fathers and their local rabbi as they grew up, but they also continued to be taught by their mothers.

The duty of educating the children was commanded by the Mosaic Law. The home became the classroom:

> These words, which I am commanding you today, shall be on your heart. You shall teach them diligently to your sons and shall talk of them when you sit in your house and when you walk by the way and when you lie down and when you rise up. (Deuteronomy 6:6–7)

This well-quoted verse instructs Jewish parents to consistently teach their children every day about the Lord and His law. We should be just as diligent in training our children.

These examples show that we, too, can be teachers to our children and have "kindness" on our tongues. Paul instructs us in Ephesians 4:32 to "be kind to one another, tender-hearted." We should begin this instruction with our own precious children. As we begin to organize our lives, taking care of and teaching our children will come much more easily.

As you teach and raise your children, there will be many times when you may think that what you are doing isn't as important as other occupations. As a grandmother now, I can certainly attest that there are times when you may feel that your life is passing you by. On the other hand, you may think that all the time and effort required to raise your children is just too hard and that you are failing. I promise you that you are not!

Let me share this quote from one of the world's best-loved preachers, Charles Spurgeon: "You are as much serving God in looking after your own children, and training them up in God's fear, and minding the house, and making your household a church for God, as you would be if you had been called to lead an army to battle for the Lord of hosts." I pray that this chapter will be a great encourager for you and motivate you into becoming the mother that God has called you to be.

Remember that kids spell love "T-I-M-E." The main reason I want us to become more organized is to give us more time for the important things in life. I hope that the following tips will help you organize the different aspects of raising your children so that you will succeed. Don't let all the suggestions overwhelm you. Pray and ask God to show you the ones you feel that He wants you to incorporate with your family.

TAKE TIME TO READ WITH YOUR CHILDREN

One of my most important goals when I was raising my children was to have at least thirty minutes every night to read with them. I guarded this goal with my life! Opportunities to bond, share, and talk with your children become rare as they get older. Reading to them will give you that time. It also will help combat the problem of illiteracy in our nation.

Recent statistics show that illiteracy is a big problem for Americans. Forty-four million adults in the U.S. can't read well enough to read a simple story to a child. As of 2012, more than three out of four of those on welfare, 85 percent of unwed mothers, and 68 percent of those arrested are illiterate. About three in five of America's prison inmates are illiterate.

This is heartbreaking. Many studies have found compelling evidence that parents make a difference in their child's reading achievement. In one, fourth grade average reading scores were forty-six points below the national average where principals judged parental involvement to be low, but twenty points above the national average where parental involvement was high. Reading to your children is simple to do, and it's free. Besides, children love it! Reading to your children every night requires turning off the television, computer, and your cell phone, but parenting requires sacrifices. If you are not sure how to start reading to your child, here are some tips (from Jefferson County Schools Communications Services).

Read to your child every day, even to tiny babies. Point to the pictures and say the names of the various objects. Point to the printed words as you read aloud. This will help them understand that words on a page have meaning, that words go from left to right, that letters make up words, and that letters have small and capital sizes.

Place soft, cloth books in your baby's crib and toy room. If they start with books from the beginning, they will always want them around.

Keep all types of books for your children within their reach. Let your children be able to reach for books on low shelves or in baskets. Be available to show them the pictures as you say what each item is. Sometimes, you don't have to actually read the book as much as saying and teaching what the items are in the pictures.

Have set times each day for reading to them. Children thrive on structure. Reading before nap time and bedtime are great times—it helps calm your child down and offers that special holding and bonding time. Also, instead of saying "bedtime," which may cause your children to get upset, say "reading time" instead. They will get ready for bed faster and without fussing when they know you will be reading to them.

Reading together every night also instills an end-of-day ritual. I think it is so important to end the day telling each child, "I love you" along with praying for them and kissing them goodnight. These little acts in a child's life can give them a huge amount of confidence, knowing there is someone in the world for them. Even to this day, I "tuck my daughters in" at night when they visit, and they are in their twenties!

As they begin to read for themselves, continue your reading with them. This is a great time to read them the classics and to expose them to different people and cultures.

Take them to the library. Get them their own library card so they can select books and magazines on their own.

Be an example by letting your children see you read. Turn off the television and spend the evening with a good book. Talk about what you have been reading. When your child sees you reading, they will learn that you value reading. You can't overestimate the value of modeling positive behavior for your children.

Have newspapers, magazines, and different types of reading materials available in your home. Talk to your children about what they are reading at home and at school. Help them decide on books for their book reports.

Play word and rhyming games. Between the ages of 4 and 7, most children begin to recognize words. They can read signs to you from the car. Ask them about the sounds of the letters in the words they are reading.

Encourage your children to write about what they have read. They could even keep a journal of the titles and authors of the books. My girls also loved to play "Library," creating a pretend library using their own books and a check-out system. They even made forms for each book where they would write their name and the date they checked out the book!

Continue reading to your children as long as they will let you. I read to my daughters into their early teens. Once they decided they were too old for that, I still had nightly prayer with them and some devotions. I have to say that when my oldest daughter said goodbye to me and walked across her college campus for the first time, I reflected how thankful I was that I had had that one-on-one time with her while she was with me. Reading to your children is just so important!

TAKE TIME TO NURTURE YOUR
CHILD'S SPIRITUAL LIFE

Keep a basket by your children's rocking chair or bed filled with devotional books you want to read to them. Before you read the usual bedtime story, start with one of these devotional stories. My children never complained about our devotional time because they thought we were just reading books.

Here are some of the devotional books I've used and my daughters have enjoyed. Kenneth N. Taylor has written some wonderful books such as *The Bible in Pictures for Little Eyes, Big Thoughts for Little People,* and *Giant Steps for Little People.* These books are excellent for children up to ages 7 or 8. Another wonderful devotional book is *The Beginners Bible: Timeless Children's Stories. Little Visits with God* by Jahsmann and Simon is a collection of everyday stories with a moral in each one.

For an older child, *The One Year Bible Storybook* by Virginia J. Muir is an excellent book for daily devotions. Each day of the year has a designated reading beginning with Genesis for January 1 and ending with the book of Revelation in December.

For teens, we used *Life Training: Devotions for Parents and Teens* by Dr. Joe White. You can find other devotionals in your local Christian book store.

Don't forget faith-oriented magazines. Focus on the Family is a great source of material for children. Both our girls received magazines according to their ages: *Clubhouse Jr.* for children ages 4-8 and *Clubhouse* for children ages 8-12.

Focus on the Family also offers *Adventures in Odyssey,* fabulous audio recordings that we took on our car trips when my children were young. These recordings have influenced the character of my children. You can also hear the *Odyssey* series on local Christian radio stations. My daughter liked to hear an episode before she went to sleep. Focus on the Family has many more videotapes and books. Check with your local Christian bookstore, or visit www.focusonthefamily.com.

Invest time in their spiritual development. Spend fifteen to thirty minutes of time with each child before they go to sleep. As I mentioned earlier, reading to them, talking to them, and praying with them is a valuable way to nurture your children's spiritual development. Divide your reading between a "Bible book" and a "pretend book." I know many families have devotions at the dinner table, which is great. But I have found that if children don't feel they are in a structured setting, they can enjoy the learning more. Before we read from a fictional book, which they could pick, we first read from a devotional book that taught the Bible. We then had family prayer time. As your children get older, teach them how to have their own Bible study time. The best way to do this is to ask them to help you with some of the questions when you do a Bible study. Also consider signing them up for the different church activities as Awana, youth groups, mission trips, etc.

TAKE TIME AFTER SCHOOL WITH YOUR CHILDREN

Spend the first thirty minutes after your child gets home from school with them. Try not to be on the phone or working on a project. Meet them at the bus or at the door. Nothing makes a child feel more special than knowing we are happy to see them.

Also, try not to talk on your cell phone while you are driving your children and their friends to activities. They are listening to every word we say and whether we realize it or not, they are learning good or bad from our conversations. Yes, it's easier to catch up on your phone calls while in the car but children should not be able to hear them. As a safety measure, whenever you do use your cell phone in the car, please use a hands-free one.

Use this time to go through their backpack, see their papers for the day, and review what homework they have for that night. I can't stress enough how important this time can be for saving time later. You'll prevent lost notes and assignments. You'll also know how much time your child should allot that day to getting homework done.

Use after-school time as a sharing and snack time together. My children seemed to want to share their day with me when we were sitting together, unhurried, after school. One of my daughters liked this time so well that as soon as she came through the door, she walked right over to our meeting place and sat down, ready to talk and go over everything. I wouldn't have traded this time with them for anything.

We have only four times to connect with our school age children each day: in the mornings before school (which is usually hurried), after school, dinner time, and right before they go to bed. Try to organize your day so every minute with each child counts.

TAKE TIME TO EAT TOGETHER AND TO TEACH HEALTHY LIFELONG HABITS

The dinner hour is one of the few times that a family can be together. This is when your children can learn communication skills with their parents and siblings. This is when you can instill your value system and it's a great opportunity to share your faith, have devotionals, and pray together. This is when you can teach your children manners. And this is when you can teach healthy habits. In the United States childhood obesity has grown considerably in recent years. Between 16 and 33 percent of children and adolescents are obese. This is a critical statistic! And although obesity is among the easiest medical conditions to recognize, it is one of the most difficult to treat. Unhealthy weight gain due to poor diet and lack of exercise is responsible for over 300,000 deaths each year.

My prayer is for families to work on providing healthy meals, eating together, and encouraging each other to exercise. These elements are crucial to living a happy and healthy life.

Begin eating together when the children are young. If you start early, it will become a good habit you'll rely on during their hard teen years. Schedule dinner time like a business appointment, even if some family members protest. They'll thank you some day for trying to keep everyone together.

If the normal dinner hour is not a good time for everyone to eat together, try changing to a later time when everyone is home. Or, if you can't eat together at dinner, try to be together at breakfast.

If you are never able to eat together, set aside one day or evening as family time. Don't let anything or anyone come in the way of this very special time. Turn off the television and all cell phones. That family time is more important than anything else.

Have a family rule that once you've served everyone and sat down, you don't get back up from the table until dinner is over. I used to hop up and down during a meal getting food or drinks for everyone. Children can learn to wait or get what they want themselves.

Try eating out occasionally, even with toddlers. No, I am not kidding! I look for creative ways to handle going out because children love it and eating out is a great way to celebrate special occasions. We even celebrate half-birthdays. If you have toddlers or very active young children, plan to dine at off-peak hours. Order as soon as you sit down and ask that the children's meals be brought out first.

Cook with your children. Families who cook together have fun! It's never too early to get your children to help with meal preparation and clean up. One of my books, *12 Steps to Becoming a More Organized Cook,* has a whole chapter entitled "Kids Can Cook, Too!" It's a great skill to teach and for them to learn. One day they will be on their own and need to know how to cook and eat healthily.

TAKE TIME FOR ACTIVITIES WITH YOUR CHILDREN

"940 Saturdays." This is the number of Saturdays between the day your child is born and the time he or she turns 18. The phrase might serve as a reminder to cherish the time you have with your child and to use it wisely. Activities with your children are a great way to begin!

Start outdoors! Children who play outdoors have been shown to be healthier, happier, and smarter. When parents and their children play together outside, everyone gets healthier. The benefits include: stronger muscles and bones; leaner body; less likelihood of becoming overweight; decreased risk of developing type 2 diabetes; possible lower blood pressure and blood cholesterol levels; better sleep; and more self-confidence and self-esteem.

Make a list of all the activities you could do together. Remember what you enjoyed as a child and make a list with your child. She will get so excited knowing that you two will be doing fun things together.

Don't forget summer and holidays. Make a list of the activities you want to do during the summer months and the school holidays. My daughters and I would make these lists, and we made a point of doing each item. When the break or summer vacation was over, we could see exactly what we did and we always felt that we had accomplished a lot.

Be their coach. If you are into sporting events, you might want to sign up as a coach for one of their teams, or the troop leader or co-leader for their scouting troop. You could also serve as a team mom for their ballet class, a helper in their church or Sunday school class, or as their homeroom mom.

Celebrate often with small activities. Even a trip for an ice cream treat can be a celebration for something special. It's time together with just Mommy. Make every day special for your children by thinking up and telling them one good thing about that day. Monday might be special because Daddy is in town. Friday may be special because it's family night. Life can be celebrated in little things every day. Doing this focuses us on the little windows of time we have with our children.

Put together scrapbooks for your children. Create your own, or use scrapbook-making as an activity for the family. The important thing is to keep a record of your children's lives for them to have when they are grown. These works of art are examples of their childhood and wonderful reminders of their roots. When I think I can't do another page, I remember my mother, who created a scrapbook for each of her seven children. That's dedication!

If you need some help making scrapbooks for your family, contact Creative Memories. This company has representatives who conduct workshops that show how to create scrapbooks. They have many beautiful books and wonderful ideas to show you. You can also design scrapbooks digitally with their software—the company will print your book for you! I have four scrapbooks of pictures of my granddaughter that my daughter designed on her computer!

You can use scrapbooks to record a variety of things:

- A photo scrapbook for all the pictures you take. Once you get hard copies of your pictures, mark the date, the names of the people, and places. Keep pictures on your desk (not in a drawer) to remind you to put them in a scrapbook.

- An individual photo scrapbook for each child. Each of my daughters has her own scrapbook with pictures that focus on her. I use plastic bins to organize extra pictures and items from their plays and events.

- A school scrapbook. This scrapbook could have sections for each school year and folders for their special papers and report cards.

- A travel scrapbook. This is a great way for your children to remember all the family trips you have taken.

If this sounds like too much, it probably is! But children love their scrapbooks and appreciate them. My daughters have always enjoyed looking through their scrapbooks and now that they are adults they still do.

Save your children's art projects from different holidays in a bag, box, or tray. When you decorate for that holiday, you can use the precious things they made when they were little. For example, each November I go down to the basement and pull out my Thanksgiving decorations. We decorate the table with construction paper turkeys, Pilgrims, and Indians my children have made through the years. One of my favorites is a cut-out turkey where my four-year-old daughter wrote what she was thankful for on each feather. She wrote the usual: food, family, etc. On the last feather, she wrote, "I'm thankful I go to the potty!" This decoration gets laughs each year and continues to be a fond family memory.

When your children are involved in an activity such as soccer or ballet, attend as many of their games or recitals as you can. Children love to have their parents cheering them on and supporting them.

Remember to take time one on one with each of your children. A child has fun at an amusement park, but rocking in a chair together or playing a sport together brings them more fulfilling love. What children like best is your undivided attention.

TAKE TIME TO HELP YOUR CHILD SUCCEED IN SCHOOL

No, I don't mean doing their homework. But you can help them develop good attitudes and habits, as well as a routine.

Talk positively about school. The way your child perceives your feeling about school and teachers will have a direct effect on how he or she feels about them.

Keep a consistent schedule. Children respond well to order. If you establish a firm pattern for school days and nights you will find yourself arguing less often about the little things. Let your children know the schedule, and the burden of responsibility will gradually shift from parent to child.

Designate a specific time for them to do their homework. This needs to be a time that works with their schedule and yours.

Provide a place that is quiet with good light, work space, and supplies. Help them develop good study habits. Encourage them to tackle the hard projects first, to plan ahead for projects, and to know that it's their homework, not yours.

Put everything in its place. Designate a place for coats and backpacks, as well as a time for you to go over their assignments and papers. The best time for this is when your children first get home. Value the work they show you and have a good attitude reviewing their work. Praise before you offer advice. Have a place designated for long-term projects that won't be disturbed while the project is being worked on.

Go to parent-teacher conferences. Get to know your children's teachers. Help in the classroom as often as you can. Statistics show that the children with the highest grades and the fewest discipline problems are those whose parents are involved with their education.

Help them get enough rest. The best tonic for sluggish mornings begins the night before. Establish a firm bedtime routine and stick to it. This is hard for working parents because they want to spend more time with their children, or feel guilty that they don't. But children need to be alert to learn. This doesn't just apply to young children, either: many teenagers have after-school jobs that keep them up too late. Help your teenagers balance the time between their job and school work. Understand that some teens need more time for homework and sleep and can't keep up with a job too.

Help them get healthy food at home and at school. Children, especially teenagers, won't eat at school if they are having fun with their friends. Make sure you teach good eating habits when they are young and explain what you are packing in their lunch. Also, ask them what they would like to have for their lunch. If you decide to let them buy at school, make sure the selections are healthy. Then, at home, provide healthy choices for their snacks. Make sure they eat a good breakfast each morning.

Keep them active—outside. Active kids aren't just healthier; they get higher grades. A study of 80,000 kids from the Delaware Department of Education found that students who performed better on fitness tests also scored higher academically and behaved better in school. Even 10 minutes outdoors can enhance your children's health.

Expect the best from your children. When our expectations are high, children have a solid goal to reach for. However, be realistic with their abilities. Not every child can make straight As. Discuss your children's capabilities with their teachers. Don't punish your children for getting Bs and Cs if this is their best.

What if your child is having trouble reading? Some children have difficulty learning to read. You may hear from a teacher that your child has difficulty with language, or you may have noticed some other difficulties. Special teaching can be given to help your child reach their full potential. There are resources available at your children's schools and libraries.

Remember that times have changed in the public school system. In the 1940s the top problems reported by teachers were such items as talking, chewing gum, and running in the halls. A similar study in 2007 showed the top problems to be drug and alcohol abuse, pregnancy, rape, suicide, and assault. (Sources: Fullerton, California, Police Department and the California Department of Education). And the newest problem, according to the U.S. National Center for Education Statistics, is school violence. They found that 5.9 percent of students carried a weapon (e.g., gun, knife, etc.) on school property; 7.8 percent of students have been threatened or injured at school, and 12.4 percent have been in a fight. These are alarming statistics!

In fact, as I'm writing this, the Sandy Hook Elementary School shooting in Newtown, Connecticut, has taken place just one month ago.

Now more than ever, we need to need to know what is going on in our children's lives and at their schools. We need to teach and show our children moral values. We need to teach them how to survive morally in today's world. These values are too important to leave for others to teach.

TAKE TIME TO DISCIPLINE AND TRAIN YOUR CHILDREN

"Train up a child in the way he should go, even when he is old he will not depart from it" (Proverbs 22:6). Parents play a large role in laying the foundation for their children's future spiritual growth and understanding. Though the challenges are many, the process is not that complex. You know how God's love changes your life. The more you communicate and model God's love for your children, the more they will grasp deeper spiritual concepts later on. As we show love to our children, it will be easier to discipline them because we'll already relate with them on a deep and sincere level.

Dr. Gary Chapman and Dr. Ross Campbell explain this process in their book *The Five Love Languages of Children*:

> Every child has an emotional tank, a place of emotional strength that can fuel him through the challenging days of childhood and adolescence. We need to fill our children's emotional tanks with unconditional love, because real love is always unconditional. Only unconditional love can prevent problems such as resentment, feelings of being unloved, guilt, fear, and insecurity. Only as we give our children this love will we be able to deeply understand them and deal with their behaviors, good or bad.

Teach your children the Ten Commandments (Exodus 20:1–17). Disciplining our children goes together with training our children. It is a constant, daily activity, totally centered on our love for them. Unfortunately, with the growing collapse of the moral environment we live in today, it is harder to discipline and train our children.

Expect your children to obey. Never forget who is the parent and who is the child. Nothing is as sad to see as a family where the children are in charge. A family is not a democracy. The parents must have the final say or everyone will be in trouble. It is important to set guidelines that encourage the Christian obedience we expect of our children. In *Dr. Dobson Answers Your Questions,* Dr. James Dobson gives valuable tips:

- Define the boundaries before you enforce them. Use common sense and make sure your child knows what you expect as far as manners, respect, and the Golden Rule.

- Explain your expectations to your children. If you know you will be driving in heavy traffic a long way, explain to your children that you need their help by being quiet and not fighting. Children respond well when we share with them what we need from them.

- If your child defies or challenges you, respond clearly and decisively. It's important to be confident when you face a nose-to-nose confrontation with your child.

- Know the difference between willful defiance and ordinary childish irresponsibility. If your child forgets to feed the dog or make his bed, remember that these behaviors are typical of childhood. If the behavior continues, then you can decide necessary consequences.

- After a confrontation is over, be sure that your child feels loved and reassured. By all means, open your arms and let him come. Hold him close and tell him of your love. Let him know again why he was punished and how he can avoid the trouble next time.

- Avoid impossible demands. Never punish him for wetting the bed involuntarily or for not becoming potty trained by one year of age or for doing poorly in school when he is trying hard.

- Let love be your guide. If there is genuine love, affection, and respect in your relationship with your child, things will work out, despite some parental mistakes and errors.

- Discipline without relationship will cause rebellion. This is an expression I heard when I was raising my children, and it is true.

Take time to plan the best punishment. Not every disobedient act deserves the same treatment. Forgetting to do a chore, in my opinion, isn't as bad as talking back to a parent and being disrespectful. And the best punishment? Taking away what they love the best. When one of my daughters was 5, she was rude at a family dinner. I took away her new bubble-gum toy and placed it on the top of the refrigerator so she could see it. She was never rude again. Another daughter, as a teenager, was rude and disrespectful to me, so her cell phone was taken away. We have to get them where it really hurts! Let your children suffer the consequences of poor behavior. If your children are arguing and fussing in the backseat on the way to an outing, turn the car around and go back home. If your teen talks back to you, don't drive him to practice. Will they get upset? Absolutely! But a teacher or a boss won't tolerate bad behavior, so you shouldn't either. To help you in this area of discipline I highly suggest the following books by Dr. Kevin Leman: *Making Children Mind Without Losing Yours; Have a New Kid by Friday*; and *Running the Rapids: Helping your Teen Survive the Turbulent Water of Adolescence.*

Never tell your child he is bad. It is only his behavior that is bad.

Treat each child as an individual. Don't favor one child over another. Don't label children by saying things like, "She's the artist in the family," or "He's the family athlete." This creates disharmony. Let your children know there is room in the family for two children to excel at the same thing.

Encourage your children to work out their own disagreements. This eases rivalry and teaches kids how to negotiate. Just say, "You have to figure this problem out yourselves. You're smart. You can do it!"

Don't solve your children's problems for them. In *Reader's Digest*, an article written by a school principal listed this as one problem she sees among parents. In fact, she says that "kids are easy. It's the parents who are tough. They're constantly trying to solve their kids' problems for them." Another term I have heard is "helicopter parents"—parents who hover over their children too much. It is very difficult to know when to help our children with their problems and when not to, and when to be right there and when not to. My suggestion is to take each day, and each child, one at a time and ask the Lord to give you wisdom to discern the best ways to help your children.

Let all your children, even the youngest, give opinions about family decisions. Every member of the family should be respected for their preferences. But remind them that Mom and Dad will make the final decisions.

Encourage imaginative play. Provide creative toys such as paints, crayons, and blank paper. Let them build their own toys in the backyard or playroom. Their play during these early years is hard work! They are forming great imaginations and work ethics when they play and create.

Be careful not to overindulge your children. The American Dream can make us feel pressured to give our children everything. But overindulgence is "the easiest way to mess up your kid," warns Jean M. Twenge, PhD, author of *Generation Me* and co-author of *The Narcissism Epidemic.* Dr. Kevin Leman, author of countless family and children books, says that giving our children too much is a form of child abuse.

Teach your children manners. Not just manners at the dinner table, but manners about being kind, giving compliments, team-playing, and making tiny sacrifices. Learning to write thank-you notes and respond graciously when others do kind things for them are important to a child's overall development. As Judith Martin says, "A polite child grows up to get the friends and the dates and the job interviews because people respond to good manners. It's the language of all human behavior."

Turn off the television! When it is on, monitor what is seen and how much time it is used. This goes for videos and games on hand-held devices too. I've seen mothers distract their young children with Disney videos for hours because it makes their life easier, and they feel the videos are better for their children than regular television programming. But the children are still sitting like zombies in front of the screen. Their little minds need to grow and develop and learn. Watching television inhibits initiative, curiosity, motivation, imagination, reasoning, and attention span. While they are watching, not one skill is being exercised.

Limit the time they spend using hand-held electronics. These weren't even invented when I first wrote this book and now that's all I see! I know children simply love these games, but I'm concerned to see 1- and 2-year-olds bent down over a tiny screen for hours. Please monitor these. Establish set times for "screen time" or limit them to weekends only. Also, children at any age should not bring these toys or cell phones to the dinner table. There ought to be at least one place in your home where true conversation—without electronics—is encouraged.

Last, evaluate your role as a parent. Instead of seeing our job as "parenting children," author and family psychologist John Rosemond says we need to return to the previous mind-set of "rearing children" or, by definition, "bringing them up." In his book *Teen-Proofing: Fostering Responsible Decision Making in Your Teenager,* Rosemond recommends setting expectations, giving them freedom to make mistakes, not making excuses for them, holding them accountable for their behavior, punishing them when they act badly, forgiving them their mistakes, and always loving them, regardless.

TAKE TIME TO TEACH YOUR CHILDREN
HOW TO BE MORE ORGANIZED

The best part of being organized is that many areas of our life will flow more freely with more available time for ourselves and others. As my life gets more organized, I am able to be a better model for my children as they learn to organize theirs. Having schedules and plans are extremely important ways of helping your children become more independent and responsible.

Expect them to help with housework and chores. Children should be contributing members of their families. First, determine what chores your child can do. Recognize the difference between a chore (an ongoing task that benefits the household) and a life skill (an activity that children should learn before living on their own). Also, remember that every child matures at a different pace. Only you know what your children's skills and talents are.

Post a schedule of chores for your children in the kitchen. You can even buy a large chart printed for this purpose.

Get your children in the habit of checking off each chore they do. Some chores are worth money. At the end of the week, have them count up what they are owed. This one tip took the responsibility of chores off me and put it onto the children. Our girls couldn't wait to do their chores so they could mark them off, knowing that at the end of the week they would see a reward. For us, this reward was their allowance. I know people have different opinions on this. I feel that allowance is as great a learning tool as regular chores are. The next point explains further.

Have some chores that must be done without pay. Kids should help around the house because they are part of a family, not solely because they get an allowance. But since we live in a world that rewards hard work with pay, our children need to learn this concept, too. They also need to learn how to handle their money. Finishing chores provides a sense of accomplishment, enlarging a child's feelings of worth. And learning how to do different chores will equip your children to live with roommates and spouses.

Children should also learn how to make their own spending money. Troy Dunn, author of *Young Bucks,* wrote this book explaining how his children are becoming more responsible and learning the value of money by earning it themselves. "Children don't respect free money," he says. "When a child purchases an item he really wants with his own money, he will take better care of the item than if someone buys it for him. We are to empower them with the ability to learn how to earn for themselves." I have heard from some parents that their children don't have time to do chores or small jobs for money because of their sports commitment. Dunn feels that sports are great but the children won't be doing sports as long as they will be working.

We should also teach our children how to handle money. They need to open a savings account when they are around 5-8 years old. They can save up their own money for this purpose. I also recommend giving them a credit or debit card and a checking account when they are 15 to 16 years of age. These will have to be linked to your own accounts: your bank can help set these up. It is so important to teach them money skills! Many young adults get into debt when they go off to college or leave home and start working. If they understand how to use money at an earlier age you will be giving them lessons that will last a lifetime.

Help them understand how to organize their own items. Remember when we tell our children to clean their rooms, our definition of that task may differ from theirs. Habits of cleanliness do not develop automatically with age. Children need neatness training. Show them how to fold sweaters, hang pants, and organize drawers. Provide special files for homework papers and projects. Children tend to keep the habits they build in childhood. Being able to organize belongings and storage space is a valuable skill they'll use all their lives.

Schedule your daily activities at a consistent time. Keep your dinner hour regular and early so that you will have the time to spend with your children in the evening. Also, avoid a giant rush by keeping breakfast and departure time the same each morning. Pray with your children each morning, or say, "God bless you today!" to them.

Have children lay out school clothes the night before. And make sure everyone agrees then! Don't argue the next morning about what they are wearing. Place book bags, papers, lunches, notes to teachers, etc., by the door so nothing will be left behind.

Keep a calendar of the family's activities posted in a place that is convenient for all to see. A magnetic calendar that attaches to the refrigerator is useful. Your children can help you schedule their activities by writing them on this calendar. It is a great tool for making sure everyone knows where everyone else is.

Keep a "no television" and "no electronics" rule on school nights. Right after dinner, you can start getting your youngest child ready for bed and reading without the fight to watch television or play Angry Birds. After you finish with that child, you will be ready for the next one. Does this take all night? Yes. I made the choice to be with my children instead of watching television when they were toddlers. I admit it was hard. But television and tablets will always be around, while children grow up all too quickly. Organizing your home and building quality relationships with the people you love takes sacrifice, but the end results are priceless. The "no screens" rule should apply also to your older children, too. They need a quiet house for homework, chores, activities, and reading.

Find out how long it takes to get your preschoolers dressed for bed or for their day's activities. Then allow them more time so you don't have to say "hurry up" so often. If your teenager is always late, tell him the time you will be leaving and make him responsible. If it's time to go and he isn't ready, leave without him or allow him to suffer some other consequence. This keeps you from nagging and teaches time management.

TAKE TIME TO DEVELOP A JOYFUL FAMILY

Joy is a word that makes us smile, sing, and dance! Yes, we should teach and discipline our children, but without joy our actions appear bland and forced. Families who laugh and play together can provide a wonderful framework in which the child can grow and develop. One reason Jesus came to live and die for us was for "[our] joy [to] be full" (John 15:11 NKJV). And joy is one of the fruits of the Holy Spirit (Galatians 6:22) showing us that God wants us to live a life full of joy.

As mothers, we need to let joy guide us. If we look for the joy in our children, we will have a powerful clue as to what is important and special to that child.

I read a story about a mother who was trying hard to get the children fed, teeth brushed, and shoes on during a busy school morning. As she walked to the door, she saw the feet of her little boy hidden underneath the coat rack. He was obviously playing hide and seek but with little time to get them to school, the mother ignored what he was doing and said, "Come on, let's get in the car!" The little boy did as he was told, but before heading for the car he said, "Mom, you didn't even laugh." Yes, getting places on time is very important, but joining in our children's joy is equally important at times.

Here are some secrets of happy families:

- Traditions. Keep them, expand them, and enjoy them. Children really love traditions and they help them feel a part of the family.

- Eating together. Children love to be with their parents, and eating together can be an unrushed special time to interact with them.

- Playing together. Whether sports, inside games, or just a pillow fight, children love just having fun together.

- Cleaning up, doing chores and errands, or cooking together. These are great opportunities to teach your children the how-to's of life as well as give them one-on-one time. And children love helping their parents.

- Being thankful. Families nurture our spiritual side by showing gratitude toward one another as well as toward the Lord.

- Physical touch. Every child loves being hugged, gentle tickling, riding horsey on your back, having their back rubbed before sleep, and holding hands.

- Laughing! Families who can laugh with each other and at each other feel bonded and happy. Happy families have private jokes only they understand. Cultivate this joy by laughing together.

- Outings or vacations. There is just something about taking a vacation for building memories. Families who invest in these are building happy ones.

- Happy family members show respect to each other. They take time to listen, allow different opinions, admit when they are wrong, and support their hobbies and team events by encouraging each other.

- Happy family members have strong communication skills with each other. They don't hold grudges.

Raising children can be difficult, and at times I wonder if I am doing anything right. I want to have my life balanced and organized well enough so that my children get my very best. And, as I have said before, the main purpose of a more organized life is to have time for your family.

TWENTY WAYS TO MAKE YOUR
CHILDREN FEEL GREAT!

1. *Show unconditional love.* This means you truly love the inside of your child—who they are, not what they do.

2. *Be careful with your anger.* Don't discipline in anger. If you are out of control, you or the child should immediately go to another room until you cool off. Do not yell unless the house is on fire.

3. *Make requests and instructions clear.* Have younger children repeat what you have just said so everyone is in agreement.

4. *Learn to listen.* Become a great listener for your child even at those times when you don't want to.

5. *Take your child's feelings seriously.* Kids remember little of what we tell them, but they never forget how we make them feel.

6. *Appreciate who your child is.* A child is a gift from God, the richest of all blessings. Find one thing about them to appreciate daily.

7. *Discipline your child with firmness and reason.* If they know you are fair, you will not lose their respect or their love. Make sure the punishment you give fits the "crime." Taking the time and effort to discipline and direct your child shows you care. This makes them feel secure.

8. *Spend time alone with each child daily.* Read to them and listen to them talk about their day.

9. *Allow your child to do things for himself.* Help them become more independent—that is our goal in raising children. Teach them there is dignity in hard work and that a useful life is a rewarding one.

10. *Respect your child's possessions.* Never go through their mail or their diaries or listen in on phone conversations. (If you suspect that they are involved with drugs or crime, talk with a professional.)

11. *Respect your child's opinions.* If you attack them when their viewpoint differs from yours, they will stop talking to you. In the growing-up years your child begins to form opinions. You are free to give your opinion and to live the life you preach; allow your child that same freedom.

12. *Understand your child's abilities.* You might have been an Olympic swimmer, but that doesn't mean your child will be. Encourage your children to try many different activities so that as they reach adulthood, they understand their strengths and interests. Don't push them into something that only you want them to do. They have their own lives.

13. *When possible, respect your children's choices.* You may have to step in when their choices involve friends you don't approve of, but try to respect their choices in clothes, music, etc. Interfere only when a choice endangers your child's welfare.

14. *Teach your children to value the health of their bodies.* At an early age, teach them the dangers of drugs, alcohol, smoking, and sexual sins. Continue talking to your older children about these dangers.

15. *Do not let your children put themselves down.* Encourage them. Build them up. Remind them that each person on earth is here for a special reason and purpose and that they are unique in the eyes of God and of you.

16. *Say "I love you" every day.* Other ways to communicate love include: a hug, a back rub, rumpling your child's hair, a kiss, letting your child sit in your lap, and spending quality one-on-one time with them.

17. ***Speak to your child at eye level.*** Let your body language show you are available to them.

18. ***Avoid double standards and mixed messages.*** Don't show favoritism. Never compare them with others who may have performed better.

19. ***Be mature enough to share your feelings and admit when you are wrong.*** Always tell your child you are sorry after a disagreement.

20. ***Teach your children to love God and others.*** Take them to a place of worship and be an example. Faith in God can be your child's strength and light when all else fails.

(With thanks to Zionsville Newsletter.)

Lo, children are an heritage of the LORD: and the fruit of the womb is his reward. As arrows are in the hand of a mighty man; so are children of the youth. Happy is the man that hath his quiver full of them.

PSALM 127:3-5 KJV

Bringing home Step 10

She opens her mouth in wisdom,
And the teaching of kindness is on her tongue.
PROVERBS 31:26

As a mother, you need to teach and lead your children with great love and kindness, and you need God's wisdom and strength in order to do this. As you take each step toward becoming a more organized woman, you'll be able to bring order to your children's lives and your home life as well.

For Further Reflection

1. What does the Bible say about the importance of children?

2. What activities do you currently do with your children? What would you like to do more of?

3. Why is spiritual nurturing often viewed as less important than social and physical nurturing?

4. What are some ways you make your children feel more special?

5. How could you help your child become a better student?

6. Are you happy with the discipline and training that you give your children? What could you change or add?

Personal Application

- Pick at least three things you could do for or with your children this week to show you think they're great and do the first one today.

- Can you think of some ways you could encourage your children with their education?

- How could you lead your children into a more real and personal relationship with God?

A WOMAN WHO WANTS TO BECOME MORE ORGANIZED . . .

Restores Herself Emotionally and Spiritually

I will refresh the weary and satisfy the faint.

JEREMIAH 31:25 NIV

Probably one of the most difficult challenges for a woman is understanding how to balance all the different aspects of her life. There are so many balls to juggle, and each aspect of our lives—being a wife, a mother, a grandmother, a sister, an employee, a friend, a neighbor, and even a Christian—comes with its own obligations.

Throughout this book, we have looked at different ways a woman can become more organized. My goal, as I have mentioned, is to help you have more *time*—time for the really important areas of your lives. I believe that as we gain more time, we will be able to restore ourselves. Only by taking care of ourselves will be able to minister to others.

However, you may be at a point in your life where you don't have the time, energy, or willpower to start taking care of yourself. I understand. So read over the following suggestions and start with just one or two tips along with prayer, asking God to help you. I promise that as you take the first step you will gain the momentum to continue.

RESTORE YOURSELF EMOTIONALLY

Our emotions are a tender part of our selves. So much can happen to our physical selves when our emotional selves have been hurt. One medical definition of emotion is: An intense mental state that arises subjectively rather than through conscious effort and is often accompanied by physiological changes. Emotions control your thinking, behavior, and actions. Emotions affect your physical body as much as your body affects your feelings and thinking.

I believe that many women today are dealing with increasing emotional stress. I don't know if it is our fast-paced lives or the huge amount of information thrown at us day and night. I don't know if more women today were abused as children or mistreated in their marriages or the work force. And I don't know if it's the "self-help" shows on TV that make us more aware of the problems we *could* have. But I do know that God wants us to be healed in every area of our lives. His Word is the balm for healing as we read and meditate on it. We just need to call upon His name: "O LORD my God, I called to You for help and You healed me" (Psalm 30:2), and believe that He can heal: "Heal me, O LORD, and I will be healed; save me and I will be saved, for you are the one I praise" (Jeremiah 17:14 NIV).

Begin to concentrate on your emotions. To realize the power that emotions can have in your life, start to examine your own emotions to see if they are acceptable to God or not. Anger, hatred, discord, jealousy, fits of rage, and selfish ambition are acts that come from the sinful nature. If you find that these emotions are taking over your life, try to find the root reason for them.

When you feel love, joy, peace, patience, kindness, goodness, faithfulness, gentleness, and self-control, these are the result of the fruits of the Holy Spirit who lives within you (see Galatians 5).

Once you become a Christian, these opposite emotions will war within you until Christ comes back. So please don't despair when your behavior is unacceptable! The apostle Paul says that the very things he wants to do he finds it hard to do, and yet the very things he doesn't want to do, he does! Because we have sin inside of us, we will battle daily. But praise be to God that He saves us daily by the blood of His Son, Jesus! Each day, confess your sins and ask the Holy Spirit to cleanse you and fill you with His strength so that you can walk in the Lord. "So I say, live by the Spirit, and you will not gratify the desires of the flesh" (Galatians 5:16 NIV).

Seek help. If you are in an abusive situation or you were abused as a child, you must find a trusted counselor that you can talk and pray with. Emotions can be pushed aside in our mind but sooner or later they will resurface. I pray you find the help you need so you can get healthy.

Let the past go. I understand that most of our emotional health comes from something that happened to us in our past. But there comes a point when we have to *let it go* to be healed. Isaiah 43:18–19 is a verse to claim if you are having trouble giving up the past: "Forget the former things; do not dwell on the past. See, I am doing a new thing! Now it springs up; do you not perceive it? I am making a way in the wilderness and streams in the wasteland" (NIV). God can heal you, and He wants to give you a new way!

Begin to make wise choices. Sometimes we have to start making new choices to get emotionally healed. Author Lysa TerKeurst has just released a new book, *Unglued: Making Wise Choices in the Midst of Raw Emotions.*

Become content. Learning to be content is a process you will need to cultivate your whole life, but great good comes from contentment. It is fine to be ambitious and set goals and dream of what you want to accomplish or purchase. But as you do that, cultivate a spirit of contentment. Paul wrote about being content *while he was in jail!* "I have learned to be content in whatever circumstances I am" (Philippians 4:11).

Restore yourself emotionally by having kindness, compassion, and generosity for others. Be true to yourself and to others. Be authentic. Have an ease about yourself of truth and honesty. Reject hostility toward others. Work at your relationships. Take care of friendships. Hold the people you love close.

Have a spirit of joy. Joy doesn't come from circumstances. Circumstances change daily. Joy comes from the inside. Cultivate a true joy of life within. It takes an act of the will to focus on the good, but as time goes by, this spirit of joy will come naturally.

Reduce the stress in your life. Stress can damage our emotional and physical lives. As you reduce the clutter in your home and life, build your relationships, work on living a healthy life, and have a daily walk with the Lord, you will be able to ease the stress in your life.

Focus on the positive in every situation. Philippians 4:8 helps to keep my mind on the right things: "Finally, brothers and sisters, whatever is true, whatever is noble, whatever is right, whatever is pure, whatever is lovely, whatever is admirable—if anything is excellent or praiseworthy—think about such things" (NIV).

And let your mind and thoughts be on the right things. We can become what we think about: "For as he thinks within himself, so he is" (Proverbs 23:7). Well-known author C. S. Lewis wrote that "we are what we believe we are." If you are discouraged, turn your thoughts elsewhere. Keep anger, bitterness, and resentment out of your thoughts: "Get rid of all bitterness, rage and anger, brawling and slander, along with every form of malice. Be kind and compassionate to one another, forgiving each other, just as in Christ God forgave you" (Ephesians 4:31-32).

Be forgiving. Unforgiveness is an emotion and an act that will do great harm. When we don't forgive others, it's as if we take poison yet expect the other person to get sick! God says He won't forgive us if we don't forgive others. Forgiving is also the antidote for resentment and anger.

Forgive yourself. Every one of us, including *all* the people of the Bible (except Christ) have failed at some point of their lives. So ask God to forgive you and then keep going, doing the best that you can. One of my favorite verses is Romans 8:1, which reminds us that "there is now no condemnation for those who are in Christ Jesus" (NIV). That means that those of us who have Christ in our hearts are not condemned for our sins. God forgives us! Isn't that wonderful?

Don't expect to look perfect. Male peacocks are resplendent creatures with lovely blue-green plumage. They are strikingly beautiful birds, but they have ugly feet! If they have imperfections, then it's OK if we do too. The media has simply wrecked our images of young women and old alike. It breaks my heart. Enjoy what you look like. Work on what you can to be healthy and strong. And don't let anyone put you down. No one criticizes the peacock! Concentrate on your own beautiful parts.

Truly know that God loves you. If you have grown up not knowing if you were loved or you don't know if you are loved today by anyone, let me emphasize that God loves you! The God of the universe and everything ever created made you for His love and joy! Please accept this truth in your heart.

Cultivate gratitude. Gratitude is one of the most important emotions in a successful and fulfilled life. When we are grateful, our focus is off ourselves and toward the Lord in thankfulness. The Psalms are full of praises and thankfulness to the Lord! Praise, thankfulness, and gratitude are so important that God says He "inhabits the praises of His people."

Melody Beattie says, "Gratitude unlocks the fullness of life. It turns what we have into enough, and more. It turns denial into acceptance, chaos to order, confusion to clarity."

RESTORE YOURSELF SPIRITUALLY

Author John Ortberg reminds us that the greatest battle of life is spiritual. We will struggle daily between the flesh of sin and the spirit of God, so restoring ourselves spiritually is of utmost importance.

Each one of us must take the time and effort to walk with the Lord every day. We must pray daily, read the Bible daily and have Christian fellowship. As you begin to do these things, you will begin to restore yourself spiritually.

Evangelist Billy Graham said,

My heart aches for America and its deceived people. I wonder what Ruth would think of America if she were alive today. She had once said, "If God doesn't punish America, He'll have to apologize to Sodom and Gomorrah." In the years since she said that, millions of babies have been aborted and our nation seems largely unconcerned. The name of Jesus is no longer allowed in prayer in many parts of our country. The farther we get from God, the more the world spirals out of control.

Ladies, we have to restore ourselves spiritually. We have to be an example to the world and to our families. If we want change in the world, it's going to have to start with us.

Put God first in your life. Ask Him to direct you daily. Only God can fully restore you. As you "seek first His kingdom and His righteousness" all those things you need in your life "will be added to you" (Matthew 6:33).

Ask God to lead and help you. "Call to me and I will answer you and tell you great and unsearchable things you do not know" (Jeremiah 33:3 NIV). God wants us to seek Him with all our heart. Ask yourself, "What brings me fullness of life?" and follow that lead.

Don't compare your spirituality with others. A young mother heard her pastor say he gets up very early every morning to spend an hour of quiet time with God. She would love to do that but her children simply will not cooperate. Instead of living with guilt, she should realize that the love she expresses to her children might "count" as a spiritual activity. She is serving God more faithfully than the very pastor who may be neglecting his wife and children in the morning so he can have that hour of quiet. Some people love to be alone so prayer time comes easily; others do not. Remember: God sees your heart and accepts your sacrifices to Him.

Be a woman of character. Fill your mind and life with thoughts and actions that honor Christ—He is actually with you in everything you do. Choose the movies, TV shows, books, and actions that will build you up as a woman as well as be an example for others.

Be honest about your sins. If you are having problems with sexual sins, such as lust, adultery, pornography; physical sins, such as alcoholism, drugs, gambling; emotional sins, such as anger, hatred, bitterness, jealousy, fits of rage—face these head on, get help, and fall on your knees before God. Your healing begins the moment you take responsibility.

God can restore your past! One of the most promising verses in the Bible is Joel 2:25: "I will restore to you the years that the swarming locust has eaten." This means that even if you are divorced, widowed, abandoned, or whatever may have happened in your life, God can and will restore the lost years back to you. I am a testimony that God can do this.

Have a thankful heart. Give thanks to God daily along with thanking your family and friends for all they do. Even if you can only think of one thing they've done, express appreciation for that one thing.

Expect great things! Anticipate the plans God has for you. " 'For I know the plans I have for you,' says the LORD, . . . 'to give you a future and a hope' " (Jeremiah 29:11). Be ready to serve the Lord every day, putting Him and your prayer life first, and you will be refreshed.

Incorporate Christian disciplines into your life. As you add these to your life, your walk with God will become your most important priority and you will become more centered, less stressed, and healthier in every area of your life. Christian disciplines include prayer, fasting, Bible study, simplicity, solitude, submission, service, and worship.

Praise God every day. This is the most powerful means of renewal. What happens when we praise God? According to Dr. Charles Stanley in *In Touch* Magazine:

- Praise magnifies God. Praise puts our focus on God, not our problems. Our thinking is wrapped in God's power, presence, and ability.

- Praise humbles us. When we worship God, we gain a right view of ourselves. Excess pride and ego are deflated. We have a healthy self-image based on God's view of who we are. By removing pride, praise strengthens us against temptation.

- Praise reveals our devotion to Christ. If we love Christ, we will praise Him. If He has first place in our life, we will honor Him with worship and thanksgiving.

- Praise motivates us to holy living. Praise opens our hearts to want to live the way God desires—holy and separated unto Him, to do His will above our own, to want to be like Him more than anyone else. The more we worship Him, the more like Him we will become.

- Praise ministers to three aspects of our life. Praise ministers to our spirit by creating humility and releasing joy. Praise ministers to our inner self by clearing our mind, calming our emotions, and setting our will. Praise ministers to our physical body by releasing tension and stress and replacing it with God's supernatural energy.

I pray that this chapter has helped you become restored in your whole being. When you are restored, you will be able to serve the Lord and others as God created you to do.

> *The LORD is my shepherd, I shall not want. He makes me lie down in green pastures; He leads me besides quiet waters. He restores my soul.*
>
> **PSALM 23:1**

Bringing home Step 11

I will restore to you the years that the ... locust has eaten.

JOEL 2:25

For Further Reflection

1. Are your emotions hurting your health?

2. What can you do or change to restore your emotions?

3. Are there hurts from your past that you can give to God and ask Him to restore those lost years to you?

4. What are some ways you could restore your spiritual life?

5. Are there some psalms you like that you could read and pray back to God as praises to Him?

Personal Application

- Take time this week to focus on how you could restore yourself emotionally and spiritually. Perhaps keep a journal of the steps you take to become whole and restored.

- If one of these steps is to talk with a counselor, make sure you find one who is dedicated to the Word of God and a Christian.

- Try taking a break—a retreat—from your everyday life to study God's Word and pray without any distractions.

A WOMAN WHO WANTS TO BECOME MORE ORGANIZED ...

Seeks the Source of Her Strength

He gives power to the weak, and to those who have no might He increases strength.

ISAIAH 40:29 NKJV

There are many books on organization—books to help you reduce clutter, simplify your life and home, and help you manage your time.

But I want to go a step further. I believe if we lay a foundation that is based on God and His principles, our life—from our relationships to our home and to our work—will all begin to come together more smoothly.

So we have to start at the beginning. We need to find the wisdom to change our lives. Proverbs 1:7 says, "The fear of the LORD is the beginning of knowledge."

This fear does not mean being afraid but rather having an awesome respect for and understanding of the holiness and power of the Lord God. If we come to Him first for help, then our foundation is strong. He will give us the wisdom and ability to put our lives in order.

As we start to change our lives, we need to ask ourselves what we are doing to grow into the image of Christ. It's only by changing into His image that we will be able to change in all areas of our lives.

First, acknowledge that you are a sinner. The Bible says that "all have sinned and fall short of the glory of God" (Romans 3:23). This verse means every single person has committed sins, making each a sinner. It is hard to acknowledge this truth, but it is true. From the time we are small, we want our own way rather than God's way. Just watch a two-year-old rebelliously tell his mother, "No!" The Ten Commandments were given to us as laws to follow but also to show us that it is humanly impossible to keep every one. We cannot keep them, so they reveal to us that we are sinners. God sent His Son, Jesus Christ, to show us another way to Him apart from the Law.

Second, understand that the penalty for being a sinner is death: "For the wages of sin is death [an eternal separation from God], but the free gift of God is eternal life in Christ Jesus our Lord" (Romans 6:23). The Old Testament teaches us that sins cause a separation between a holy God and us: "your iniquities [sins] have made a separation between you and your God, and your sins have hidden His face from you so that He does not hear" (Isaiah 59:2). Since we are separated from God because of our sins, God sent His Son, Jesus Christ, to restore us to Him.

Our sins also cause a separation between people too. Because of our sinful nature, relationships break. Bringing Jesus into our lives to take our sins away and restore us to God will also open our hearts and restore our relationships to our husbands, our children, our friends, and our extended family.

Third, realize that God is a God of great love. His desire is to have a loving relationship with us: "For God so loved the world, that He gave His only begotten Son, that whoever believes in Him shall not perish, but have eternal life" (John 3:16). God had a great plan to bring you and me to Him. God substituted Christ's perfection and purity for our imperfection and sin through Christ's death, burial, and resurrection: "Christ . . . suffered once for sins, the righteous for the unrighteous, to bring you to God. He was put to death in the body but made alive in the Spirit" (1 Peter 3:18 NIV). Jesus took away our sins, brought us back into a relationship with God, and gave us a free gift of eternal life. Personally, I couldn't bear to live this life not knowing if I would ever see my family again after I die. I am amazed that some women will not talk about whether or not they will be going to heaven. But how could anyone not want to know for sure? The Bible says clearly that if we believe in Him we will not die but will have eternal life. Because of Jesus, I will see my family again!

Fourth, know that He gave us the right to become one of His children: "But as many as received Him, to them He gave the right to become children of God, even to those who believe in His name" (John 1:12). We actually are heirs to everything that is God's! And what a comforting thought to any woman who never had a father or never had a good relationship with her father. God says He will be the father to the fatherless. He wants to hold you in the "hollow of His hand" (Isaiah 40:12). What a wonderful thought!

Fifth, Jesus is standing at the door to your heart, waiting for you to ask Him in. "Behold I stand at the door and knock; if anyone hears My voice and opens the door, I will come in to him and will dine with him, and he with Me" (Revelation 3:20). This is a great promise God gives to us. If you have never opened the door for Jesus to come into your life, then pray and ask Jesus to come into your life right now. Or, if you asked Him years ago and are ready to recommit your life to Him, now is the time to right yourself before the Lord. This is such an important step because He can guide you and give you the strength you need in living every day.

Sixth, know that Jesus is who He says He is and is alive! The good news of the gospel is that it is true. It is not rooted in mythology or legend but in verified fact, and it's the greatest story ever told. Paul wrote that the most important event in human history—the resurrection of Jesus Christ—is supported by actual eyewitnesses. While listing disciples who had seen the risen Christ, Paul added a list of eyewitnesses: "He was seen by over five hundred brethren at once, of whom the greater part remain to the present, but some have fallen asleep" (1 Corinthians 15:6 NKJV). At the time Paul wrote this, many of those witnesses were still alive and available for questioning. You have a God who is alive and working in your life every single day to give you a hope and a life. You also have a God who "will never leave you [nor] forsake you" (Hebrews 13:5).

To live the Christian life, to be a loving woman who can really make a difference in the lives of her family and friends, you must have supernatural strength and help from God. Jesus said, "Apart from Me, you can do nothing." Because we are all sinners, the only way to live a life that is full of love, joy, peace, patience, kindness, goodness, faithfulness, gentleness, and self-control is to live a life that is controlled by God's Spirit. And His Spirit comes into our lives when we ask Jesus into our life. Only by His Holy Spirit can any of us live a godly life. We cannot do it by ourselves.

As the Holy Spirit leads, you will also realize that many negative emotions need to be removed from your life. One of these is worry. As children of God, we can give Him all of our worries! As Corrie ten Boom said, "Worry does not empty tomorrow of its sorrow; it empties today of its strength."

Ask yourself if you have ever really given your whole heart and soul and life to the Lord. Confess your sins to Him and then ask Him to take over your life and be your God: "If you confess with your mouth Jesus is Lord and believe in your heart that God raised Him from the dead, you will be saved; for with the heart a person believes, resulting in righteousness, and with the mouth he confesses, resulting in salvation" (Romans 10:9–10). Once you have asked the Lord Jesus into your life, you will have His Spirit living within you to guide you, direct you, and give you supernatural strength. Only with His strength can we live the Christian life.

God can also take away any guilt about the past and can make you brand new inside: "Therefore if anyone is in Christ, he is a new creature; the old things passed away; behold, new things have come" (2 Corinthians 5:17). When this guilt is lifted by God, you will have new strength, new hope, and new abilities to manage and cope with your life. This is such a blessing! Once you have given your life to the Lord, here are some tips to help you grow.

BEGIN TO GROW AS A CHRISTIAN

Relationships never stay the same. They either get better or worse but they never stay the same. This also goes for your relationship with God. Just as we need to spend time with our loved ones to keep the relationship strong, we need to spend time with God.

To grow as a Christian you need to have Christian fellowship, sound teaching, personal prayer, and devotions. Here are some ideas to help you.

FIND THE RIGHT CHURCH

It's important for you to have fellowship with other believers. Find a church where the Bible is taught and where your children will learn and grow through Sunday school and other programs.

Look for a church close to your home. You will want to spend more time at your church if it is nearby than if it is far away.

See if your church has a weekly Bible study where you could begin to learn about God's Word and grow as a godly woman. If not, ask if they know of any neighborhood Bible studies. There are several good ones available nationwide:

- Stonecroft Ministries (Friendship Bible Coffees)
- Bible Study Fellowship

- CBS—Community Bible Study

- Precept upon Precept Bible Studies

- Beth Moore's Bible studies

PLAN FOR A FRUITFUL PRAYER TIME

Begin each day with prayer, asking God to help you be an organized and godly woman. Some women only have time for one-sentence prayers. But try to schedule time during the day when you can pray with the Lord and read His Bible. The way I did this was to make a place in my home where my Bible and devotionals are located. I go there the same time every day to read and pray. It doesn't have to be a fancy place. Mine is a quiet corner of my bathroom. What is important is to make a place and a time to be alone with your heavenly Father.

Buy a daily devotional book. Some of these daily readings will only take a few minutes but will help you to focus on God each day. Only through His strength can we accomplish anything. Philippians 4:13 promises us that we will be able to "do all things through Him who strengthens [us]."

Ask God to give you a special love and attitude so that the climate of your home is positive, uplifting, and fun. You can choose whether your loved ones will feel loved or not. Give as much love out as you can.

Clear out your spiritual rooms. Just as you can go through your house room by room to see what needs to be organized and cleaned, so you should also go through the rooms in your heart, soul, and spirit, seeking what should be organized and cleaned, and what needs to go or stay. Make your spiritual house ready for the Lord to live there.

Writing this book has given me so much joy and I am praying daily that whoever reads it will be blessed in her body, soul, and spirit. I also pray that your life will become full and abundant, for Jesus came that we might have life—and life abundantly!

May you put the Lord first in your life, love Him with all your heart, all your soul, and all your might; and may His love pour through you to the many others He has given you in this life. I pray that your life will be a blessing to you as well as a blessing and an example to others as you step toward becoming a more organized woman.

> *He who has begun a good work in you will*
> *complete it until the day of Jesus Christ.*
>
> **PHILIPPIANS 1:6** NKJV

Bringing home Step 12

I can do all things through Him who strengthens me.

PHILIPPIANS 4:13

For Further Reflection

1. What is the foundation in your life?

2. What does it mean to "fear the Lord"?

3. Where does the strength to do it all come from?

4. Can God take away any guilt you might have from anything you might have done or not done (see 2 Corinthians 5:17)?

5. What steps can you take to ask God to be in your life?

Personal Application

- If you want God to be in your life, then pray right now for Him to forgive you of your sins and to come into your heart.

- If you have already asked God to be a part of your life, are you having a daily quiet time with Him including prayer and Bible reading? Are you attending a church and having fellowship with other believers? These steps are vital for you to grow as a Christian. May God bless you as you grow.

ABOUT THE AUTHOR

Lane Jordan is a best-selling author, international motivational and inspirational speaker, recording artist, Bible teacher, Certified Professional Life Coach with the American Association of Christian Counselors (AACC), a member of the Advanced Writers and Speakers Association (AWSA), wife, mother, and grandmother. She attended Auburn University, where she studied fashion merchandising and marketing. She then transferred to Georgia State University and graduated with a Bachelor of Arts degree in journalism and broadcasting.

She served as the associate producer for the weekly television program *In Touch* with Dr. Charles Stanley and was the editor of the First Baptist Church of Atlanta's weekly newsletter, *The Witness.*

Lane was born and raised in Atlanta, Georgia, in a family of seven children. As a child, she enjoyed gymnastics, cheerleading, piano, and scouting. As an adult, along with her love for reading, writing, and singing, Lane enjoys decorating and sports, especially tennis, golf, swimming, walking, and hiking. She also loves all types of needlework and has begun oil painting again.

Lane began speaking and writing over twenty years ago while she was living in Littleton, Colorado. She now lives in Frisco, Texas, with her husband, Scott, who partners with her in ministry. Along with Scott, her family consists of daughter Christi and son-in-law Mike and their daughter Sara; Katie; and Grace.

Lane's heart's desire is to do all she can for the Lord and to love, support, motivate, and encourage women in all walks of life.

She has written four books, all on the subject of helping women become more organized. She also released a collection of well-known, contemporary gospel songs titled *How Do I Live?*

Currently, Lane writes a weekly blog to help inspire and motivate women in all aspects of their lives. You can find this blog at: www.pathwaystoorganization.com.

If you are interested in having Lane Jordan speak to your church or organization for seminars, workshops, retreats, special events, or media appearances, you may contact her at:

lane@lanejordanministries.com

or

www.lanejordanministries.com